PARCELLS

PARCELLS

Autobiography of the biggest Giant of them all

Bill Parcells
with Mike Lupica

Bonus Books, Chicago

91   90   89   88   87   5   4   3   2   1

Library of Congress Catalog Card Number: 87-71255

International Standard Book Number: 0-933893-40-X

Bonus Books, Inc.
160 East Illinois Street
Chicago, Illinois 60611

Typography: Point West, Inc.

Printed in the United States of America

For Mickey Corcoran,
the Jersey guy who made all the difference
for this Jersey guy

CONTENTS

Foreword

It's only an act of common decency that my friend Walter gives me first shot, because if it hadn't been for me, there would have been no Super Bowl championship in his life. I saved the son of a bitch's life.

Walter? That's what I've called Bill Parcells ever since the days when we were young coaches together at West Point. I met him in the 1966–67 season, my third year as head coach. He had just joined the staff of head football coach Tom Cahill as an assistant, but I knew of him before that because he had played for my friend, Mickey Corcoran, in high school.

It wasn't long after I had met him that I knew for sure he was a basketball fan, and I was a football fan so our interests made us good friends right from the start.

We spent a lot of evenings talking about coaching and working with kids while we were together at West Point. Since then, I have visited with him at almost every place he has coached, up to and including his present role with the Giants. I have always kept in touch with him by phone, and of course I have really enjoyed watching him progress.

When I first talked with him, I understood what a great grasp he had on coaching—not coaching football, but coaching period. He knew even then that a very big part of coaching is developing a winning attitude with your players. I knew he would be an outstanding teacher, because of his attention to detail. He was always very complete with his preparation and very analytical after games.

And, win or lose, he would take the same kind of approach in setting up the next game.

His whole philosophy is built around the fact that you have to be able to stop people with your defense before you can hope to be any good. I have to like that, since that always has been paramount in my own thinking as a coach. I don't use the word defense when I talk to him. I always tell him, "You've gotta guard those guys... Are you guarding anybody yet?"

And I'll say this: From what I've seen, nobody guards them any better than the Giants with guys like Lawrence Taylor, Harry Carson, Carl Banks—and Bill Parcells.

He used to come to our practices at West Point, and he went on some recruiting trips with me. Occasionally he would go on a road trip with us and sit on our bench. *I* had to tell *him* to keep quiet. At that time, I had enough problems on my own. I had to keep *his* fat ass on the bench.

I wasn't always successful. I remember we were playing South Carolina in the NIT at Madison Square Garden, and he was sitting on the bench with us. We made a good play, he threw an arm forward, and his sport coat came up over his head. It almost strangled him—I really believe it would have if his old buddy Bob hadn't stopped coaching his team and taken the time to go get him untangled. I can see that coat still—glen plaid, black and white, with a thin red strip in it.

And the Walter part?

That goes back to West Point, too. There used to be a high school basketball talent scout in New York named Walter November. Parcells loved that name. That's what I've called him ever since.

I have called him some other names when he was winning a football game and dropped his team back in that damned prevent defense. This past year, the championship season, when everybody was patting him on the back, I told him they were hitting him just a little bit above the right place to stick that prevent defense.

Then this year, for the first time, we started playing a little zone defense at Indiana. With all those things I had said to him about his prevent defense, I had set myself up pretty well for him. And he did let me have it.

I was really pleased and honored that he asked me to come out to see the Super Bowl. I would have liked nothing more than to have been there, on his greatest day—so far. But I really couldn't. We were right in the middle of our own Big Ten season then, and I know he understood.

So, I had to watch him win it on TV, and, boy, was that hard on me. There isn't anything I find harder in the fall than watching the Giants play on TV. I root so hard for them it's like my own team is playing.

If somebody were to ask me my opinion of Bill, there are two things I would say: No. 1, the son of a bitch can really coach, and No. 2, nobody has ever had a better friend than he has been to me.

I've been around the Giants' locker room. I've watched them on the field. I know the kind of respect they have for him and for what he has put together. If he has the perseverance to stay around long enough, I feel very sure that he will go down as one of the all-time great coaches.

As for Mike Lupica, I think my feeling about sportswriters is pretty well known, but he happens to be in the minority who understand what they're doing. I can only figure that it has come from great guidance he has gotten from patient, tolerant, understanding coaches like Parcells and me.

Bob Knight
Head Coach
Indiana University Hoosiers

1 •

Super
Sunday

The morning of Super Bowl XXI, I woke up at 5:36 in a Howard Johnson's about twenty minutes from the Rose Bowl and took a regulation shower.

If the day went well, my next shower would be with Gatorade in thirteen hours or so. I'd get that one if the Giants beat the Broncos. It would be given to me by Harry Carson, who'd become the most famous shower attendant in America by then.

I'd never been quite so interested in personal hygiene my whole life.

I'm a Jersey guy. It's reality, not a cute line. I'd grown up in Hasbrouck Heights, maybe five minutes from where they ended up building Giants Stadium. I'd grown up a Giants fan. I'd gone to games in the Polo Grounds, when they still played there, and at Yankee Stadium. I'd listened to the 1956 championship game against the Bears—

last time they'd won the whole thing—on the radio. And I'd died along with everybody else when they lost to the Baltimore Colts in sudden death in 1958.

So I brought my own history with me to Super Bowl XXI, some old, some new. The new had to do with my Giants. We had won eleven games in a row. We hadn't lost since the 19th of October, when the Seahawks beat us. We'd had everything break right in the playoffs, and beaten the 49ers and Redskins by a combined score of 66-3. If we finished running the table against the Broncos, I could go home to Jersey, to the stadium five minutes from Hasbrouck Heights and give Giants fans a homecoming present they'd been dreaming about for thirty years.

At 5:36 in the morning at Howard Johnson's, I was not thinking it was just another Sunday. I'd started coaching at Hastings College in Hastings, Nebraska, in 1965, after a college career at Wichita State that fell somewhat short of the Heisman Trophy. I'd been coaching ever since, except for one year in my life later on that I'll tell you about. I'd been a football gypsy and turned my wife and daughters into gypsies too. I'd gone from Hastings to Wichita State to West Point to Florida State to Vanderbilt to Texas Tech. Just when I thought I had a terminal case of assistantitis, I became head coach at Air Force.

Then I was out of football, then back in with the New England Patriots, then to the Giants as an assistant and finally head coach.

I became Ray Perkins' assistant with the Giants in 1981. The five minute trip from Hasbrouck Heights to Giants Stadium had only taken me sixteen years.

Now it was Super Bowl XXI and the Rose Bowl and my guys were playing for everything.

Maybe Harry and I would get together for one of those nationally televised showers that had become the hallmark of another Giants victory.

Maybe.

The first thing I did at Howard Johnson's was walk to the window and check out the weather. The kickoff wasn't until 3:13 in the afternoon. But I was already coaching.

Wasn't just another Sunday.

Or just another game.

W̲e hadn't worked out at the Rose Bowl on Saturday. It had more to do with superstition than anything else. When we lost to the Seahawks, we'd worked out at the Kingdome the day before. When we lost our opener to the Cowboys, we'd worked out at Texas Stadium the day before.

And that had been it for the Giants, loss-wise.

The players thought it was their superstitions that kept us out of the Rose Bowl. Actually, it was the *coach's.* I am superstitious as hell, always have been. Ask anybody who knows me. If I'm driving in the car and I see that I've crossed a black cat's path, well, we just throw it into reverse, *re-cross* the path, and then we continue our trip.

It was my Italian mother, bless her soul, who told me about that one.

My position was: You don't mess with superstitions—from an Italian mother or otherwise—the day before the Super Bowl.

So I wake up thinking about a stadium I've never been inside and a field I've never seen except on television. I've talked to Herb Welch, one of our safeties, about it; when he was at UCLA, they'd played home games at the Rose Bowl. He'd told me the field was good but the corners of the end zone were close, so you had to watch out for the stands if you ran any corner patterns. And John Robinson, a friend who coached the Rams and had coached USC *in* the Rose Bowl, told me the field itself had a tendency to get a little oily.

You wanted to know about my day? I'm staring out the window and looking at morning haze and wondering about close end zone corners and an oily field, and the kickoff is more than nine hours away. It was my version of California dreaming, okay?

I'd told our trainer Ronnie Barnes I'd meet him in the coffee shop at 7:30. I always meet Ronnie before road games, and we take a cab to the stadium together. I'm as close to Ronnie as anybody in our organization. He's more than a trainer, more like my sidekick, Butch Cassidy or something. He is loyal, tireless, and fulfills one of the number one obligations of a true friend: He knows when to talk and when to shut up. And he knows me. When I say 7:30 to Ronnie that means 6:45 in the coffee shop for breakfast and 7:30 *on the curb,* getting into the cab.

In the biggest game of everybody's life, we weren't about to change the program.

I'd thought about putting on a suit and tie. Super Sunday and all that. Formal occasion. Dress up like I was going to church. Then I thought, Hell with that. Parcells in a suit and tie? Ronnie Barnes would have gone into a dead faint. So would anybody else who knew me and happened to be prowling the lobby at dawn's early light.

I put on my warmup suit and sneakers.

I couldn't get the field out of my mind, so I knew the first thing I was going to do when we got there was walk the field.

Ronnie was in the coffee shop waiting for me, which was no upset. He had the *Los Angeles Times,* that whole stack of it, on the table in front of him. He was reading the sports section, and without saying anything he started to offer it to me.

I said, "Pass."

Ronnie smiled.

"There's the usual pile of crap in there about the game," he said. "You sure we're playing in the same game they're writing about?"

I fooled with a cheese danish—last thing I'd eat on Super Sunday—and some coffee and Ronnie just sat there grinning at the *LA Times* sports section, humming to himself. He hums when he's nervous. Occasionally, he'd read me a little piece of something. Jim Murray, the *Times* columnist, referred to the Giants as a motorcycle gang, which we got a kick out of, because what I mostly thought about us was a bunch of guys carrying lunch-pails. With a few superstars sprinkled here and there.

"You nervous?" Ronnie said.

"I'm just worried about that Elway."

Ronnie, who's bright and funny enough to be an uncle to the Cosby kids, said, "Hell, we're going to chase

John Elway out into the parking lot before it's over."

I wasn't sure about all that, but it made the danish go down a little easier while Ronnie hummed and read and hummed.

Before we left, Ron Erhardt came in. He's our offensive coordinator now, and he'd been my boss once with the Patriots, when he was head coach there. He'd also been a great college coach at North Dakota State. Fargo, we call him.

I asked him how the quarterback meeting had gone the night before. Ron had spent about thirty minutes with Phil Simms and Jeff Rutledge.

"Phil's ready," Erhardt said. "He's glad we're gonna come out throwing."

I said, "He better be."

Then I asked him about Rutledge for some reason. Maybe I was being clairvoyant. Because little did I know that Rutledge would make the biggest decision of the game on a fourth-and-one later on, and maybe gain our biggest yard of the season.

Erhardt said, "You know you never have to worry about Rutledge."

Ronnie and I were ready to go. I got up, shook hands with Erhardt, who'd given me my shot in the pros when the pros weren't exactly kicking my door in.

"Well," I said, "it's just like the North Dakota State-Augustana game, right?"

"I think," Ron Erhardt said, "it's a little bigger than that."

Ronnie and I got into the cab at 7:30 on the button. Game plans are game plans.

When we got to the Rose Bowl, the guard wouldn't let us get anywhere near the stadium. We didn't figure we'd have a lot of trouble with this at eight in the morning, but now Ronnie is fumbling for credentials and he's yelling at the guard and the guard is yelling back. I roll down my window and smile.

I'll handle everything.

The guard says, "Who are you?"

"I'm Bill Parcells, the Giants coach."

"Right."

We end up having to walk the last block. As we get out of our cab, another cab pulls up right in back of us, and Joe Morris gets out. Our little big man. I'd nearly started the season without him because of his holdout, but he finally worked it out about an hour before the Cowboys game. And now here we were at the Rose Bowl, nearly five months later.

At eight o'clock in the morning.

"Where the hell have you been?" I said to Joe Morris.

Joe and Ronnie went to the locker room. I went to the field. Okay: I'm guilty of being a weather fanatic on game day. *Any* game day. Two weeks before, when we'd played the Redskins in the NFC Championship game, I'd gotten to my office about the same time of day and started calling Newark Airport and the National Weather Bureau because of high winds. I wanted to know what those winds were going to be like when the ball was kicked off.

If the weather channel had been a call-in show, I would have called one of those weather girls and asked her.

If I'd had home phone numbers, I would have called meteorologists.

It is not exactly a news bulletin that football coaches are a little crazy.

So I walked the Rose Bowl. I looked around, thinking, you could fit the whole football stadium at Hastings College into one little section of the stands here.

Then came a quick, spot quiz:

Where's the sun going to be at three?

(I don't want my receivers looking into the sun in the first quarter.)

Any wind?

(None. No wind, no factor.)

What about the end zones?

(Herb Welch was right on the money. Anybody who caught a touchdown pass in the corner was going to be catching one in a phone booth.)

So, how's the field?

(The field was *magnificent*.)

I don't know what I expected for the locker room at a Super Bowl, but I was amazed at how tiny ours was. I sort of expected a suite at the Plaza Hotel and got the maid's closet. Our equipment in the main part was stacked up like sardines. There was a coaches' room in the back, but it wasn't anything you would have described as opulent. The training room consisted of two benches. I figured the players would be all right, but I was also thinking ahead to all the other people who'd be in there later on, people from the organization and so forth, and I had this vision of a New York subway car at rush hour.

Morris was already in gray sweats.

"You're not ready to go, are you?" I said.

"Not at all, no sir, not me," he said.

And we just sat there and talked for half an hour about nothing. He talked about what it was like to run the ball at Syracuse, where Jim Brown had run the ball and the late Ernie Davis and Jim Nance and Larry Csonka. Joe—who's five-foot-seven and built like a jeep—told me how he'd started off at guard in high school and then moved to quarterback.

He said, "Three passes a game, tops, and I couldn't even complete them."

Nothing about the game.

It could have been any empty locker room that either one of us had known in our football careers. Joe's not real chatty before a game and neither am I, but there was still so much time to go and we wanted to fill up a little of it with small talk. Finally he ran down and so did I.

"We're going to come out throwing," I said.

Joe said he knew that.

"We want to loosen them up right at the start."

He nodded.

"But we're eventually going to get around to you," I said. "And you know I've been on your ass all week about goal-line plays and short-yardage stuff. When we get there, you're going to get the damn ball and I want you to *protect* the damn ball and don't let them make momentum by stopping us."

Historically, the Broncos were great on third-and-one, third-and-two. They'd made quite a few plays during the season in those situations, and changed games around.

"Hey, this is important," I said.

And Joe Morris said, "I know it."

Joe made seven yards on the first third-and-one situation in the game.

It's about 9:30 now, and some of the offensive linemen—Chris Godfrey, Brad Benson, Bart Oates—show up. Then Simms is there. Simms, of course, is delighted with the game plan. But I know the offensive linemen aren't. They want to just go out there and pound them a while before we open things up. They want to get a feel, dig in, establish their own foothold. But now they know the stress is going to be on them early.

If Simms gets sacked, they look bad.

None of us realize it at the time, but Simms will go out later and throw the football equivalent of a perfect game at the Denver Broncos. He'd nearly Don Larsen them. We don't know that, and we certainly don't want to know about a practice Simms had had ten days before, when he'd looked as bad as I'd ever seen him. He was throwing awful, the receivers were dropping the balls he did get near them—a nightmare. It was the Wednesday before we left for California.

Before the end of practice that day, I'd pulled Phil aside and said, "Could you do me one favor? Could you complete one stinking pass before we finish today so I can sleep tonight?"

He did. Then he was perfect the next day, and nearly perfect every day after that. Little did I know: As the Giants finished running the table on the season, Phil Simms would do the same thing. After a while in Super Bowl XXI, he wouldn't miss a ball.

In the locker room Simms said, "Let's get after them early."

I said, "Don't worry, we're going to."

We *were* going to. We'd played the Broncos earlier in the season at Giants Stadium, and I felt we were lucky to win 19–16. John Elway scared the hell out of me then; he scared the hell out of me now. It was mostly because of his improvisational skills; you can do everything right against Elway, by the numbers, just like you wanted to all week in practice, and then he dances a little and sprints over there and throws one down the field fifty yards and you lose, pal.

We'd also played cautiously at Giants Stadium. The offense hadn't done anything until the end, when Phil hit Bobby Johnson on third-and-twenty-one and then hit Phil McConkey for forty-six yards.

So I didn't want to hear about big point spreads or anything else. I felt that if we played cautiously again, we would lose Super Bowl XXI.

No matter what the oddsmakers were saying—they know more than me?—I felt the sides were even.

Simms wandered off and I got some coffee. He and I don't talk an awful lot before games. He knows my moods and I know his pretty well after all this time. He's come to know I think he's the best, especially for our team. He is a stand-up guy. He takes the heat. He takes criticism; God knows he's heard enough of it from Giants fans.

And me.

I think, If he throws 55 percent, hits a couple of big plays, we can win.

Repeat: Little did I know.

And I knew the morning would eventually end, even

if it already felt like it had lasted two days. The first team bus shows up and then the second team bus, and it's getting near noon, but not near enough, and now I'm worrying about the guys we've got on Injured Reserve.

Let me back up.

We've got seven guys in Injured Reserve who aren't going to play: Terry Kinard, who'd been our starting safety, Tyrone Davis, Jeff Hostetler, Curtis McGriff, George Adams, John Washington, Vince Warren. On Friday night, Tom Power, who's the Giants Director of Promotions, sends Jimmy Madaleno, an assistant trainer, up to my room. I'm sure Power was afraid to come himself; I kidded him about it afterward.

Jimmy Madaleno tells me it's an NFL rule, no Injured Reserve guys on the sideline for the Super Bowl.

I took it well.

"Bullshit," I said to Madaleno.

Now we've had a smooth Super Bowl week up to then. Practices have gone very well, we've handled the media stuff very well in my opinion, nobody's gotten hurt, nobody's gotten arrested. Now I've got a problem, because these guys are part of the team, and I know I'm going to get them on the sidelines, one way or another, no matter what the league says.

And obviously the word is spreading.

My phone rings. It's Curtis McGriff. Hurt defensive end with hurt feelings.

Curtis: "Is it true?" He doesn't even have to say what the subject is; he assumes we both know.

Me: "It's true right now. But I'm working on it."

Jeff Hostetler calls next. He's my No. 3 quarterback usually, he does some work on special teams and even at wide receiver, and he's a little more irate than McGriff.

Hostetler: "Hell, Bill, we're a part of the team, we practice with the team, it's the damn *Super Bowl.*"

Me: "I agree with you."

Hostetler: "Huh?"

Me: "I'm working on it."

Actually, Ricky Sandoval was working on it, which meant nobody had to worry for a minute.

Ricky Sandoval works for a company called Contemporary Services, an events management firm based in southern California. He's twenty-seven years old, six-foot-four, about 330 pounds, a dark, extremely handsome Hispanic kid. And he's become my hero during Super Bowl week. The first day we get to the Westin South Coast Plaza in Costa Mesa—we didn't move to the Howard Johnson's until Saturday—Ricky introduces himself and tells me he's from Contemporary Services and the league has assigned him to me. I asked him about ten questions in the next minute, and he smiles and answers all of them.

"How you gonna keep people off the players' floors?"

Ricky Sandoval says, "Coach, it's taken care of." And tells me how.

"I don't want anybody on the second floor, where the Giants offices are gonna be."

He says, "Coach, I'll take care of it."

And Ricky Sandoval is perfect the whole week. Every time I ask him for anything, he tells me it's already taken care of. If we were in the lobby and somebody started to bother one of the players, there was Ricky Sandoval.

Ricky Sandoval is to security what my linebackers are to linebacking.

If he drops sixty or seventy pounds, I'm ready to move him in behind Harry Carson in the 3-4 defense.

I get off the phone with Hostetler on Friday night and I call Ricky. I tell him I've got a problem with league rules and Injured Reserve guys.

He says, "Coach, I don't believe I've heard of those rules."

I love him a little more.

"We'll get some extra security passes," he says.

I tell him I expect some league guys to be on the sideline, or at least near the entrance where we come out of the tunnel and onto the field.

"Coach, I'll take care of it. If not, give them the passes from the assistant coaches and I'll make sure the assistant coaches get on the field."

On Sunday, Ricky shows up on the first bus. Now we haven't talked about our little problem much on Saturday, because I just assume Ricky is handling it. Ricky, I figure, could handle problems of national security. He comes up to me in the locker room and says, "Let's take a walk."

We got to the end of the tunnel, and standing on each side of the entrance are two black kids who look like they could be linebackers for me too. They're not as big as Ricky, but big enough.

Ricky smiles and says, "They're with me."

I started to tell the two kids about the injured players and Ricky holds up a hand.

"Coach, you just point them out when it's time. And, Coach: If they kick them off, we'll just wait a while and let them back in."

It turns out the two new kids are from Yonkers.

As I turn to go back into the locker room, one of them says, "Coach, we're Giants fans. Beat the hell out of those guys."

Giants fans are everywhere, I keep finding out.

The rest of it from before the game is just snapshots:

—I came back into the locker room and found Lawrence Taylor lying on the floor, flat on his back, like he was sleeping. It was par for the course. Lawrence likes to get to the locker room late, take it very easy, then get more and more animated as the game gets closer. By the time we take the field usually, the voice you hear is LT's.

I looked at him and smiled. The previous spring he'd checked himself into a drug treatment program. To this day a lot of people think I got him into rehab. Wrong. Lawrence Taylor isn't the only Giant who's been in rehab. Some of the others I did take by the hand. But Lawrence did it himself. And even before he played a minute in Super Bowl XXI, he'd come all the way back to being as great a player as he'd ever been for the Giants.

From the floor of the maid-closet locker room, he saw me and winked.

I wasn't worried about LT.

—I told Phil McConkey to go find out where the Giants fans were sitting, and to whip them up when we took the field.

Now McConkey is one of my wide receivers, and returns punts. If things broke right, he was going to be important against the Broncos, as he'd been in our first meeting. I'd cut him before the season, then got him back in a trade with Green Bay after Lionel Manuel went down against the Saints in the fourth game of the regular season. It was then that McConkey produced one of my favorite football quotes ever. I'm prejudiced because it came from one of my guys, but I think it belongs in that Bartlett's Familiar Quotations.

McConkey: "The grass is always greener my *ass.*"

I thought that summed up coming back to the Giants nicely.

McConkey had been a Navy helicopter pilot in Vietnam. He was tough as hell, and the biggest ham on the team. The gold medal winner. I'm not even sure who silver and bronze were, McConkey was so far out in front. He *loved* the spotlight. And he's great at working a crowd. Sometimes he would stand up on our bench during games at Giant Stadium and start waving a white-and-blue towel, and it wasn't in surrender, because pretty soon the joint was jumping.

When we ran out on the field after the introductions, McConkey grabbed a towel, ran to the section like I told him, and began waving like a sonofabitch.

We were a long way from home, but the noise sounded very familiar. Very Jersey.

—Then there was Neil Diamond and me.

Couple of Giants fans talking about the big game.

I always stand on the fifty-yard line before the coin toss, with Harry Carson on my left. Another superstition. So there I was on the fifty-yard line at the Rose Bowl, a few minutes before the one game you dream about your whole career, but never know if you're going to have. There were bands, color, noise. The sidelines were full of people. Again: There I was. I'd been 3–12–1 my first season as head coach of the Giants. If Giants general manager George Young could have convinced Howard Schnellenberger to take my job (Schnellenberger was an old friend of George's, and he was about to win a national championship at the University of Miami), I would've been out of work. In 1979, I was out of football completely because my family needed me more than football did, and my only contact with pro football had been sitting in the stands at Mile High Stadium and watching—you guessed it—the Denver Broncos play.

My first official move as head coach was to bench Phil Simms.

I'd nearly lost Lawrence.

Now there I was. On the sideline, someone bumped into me, and I looked and saw it was Neil Diamond, who was going to sing the National Anthem. Diamond looked more nervous than I felt.

I said, "Tell you what, Neil. I'll go out there and sing the National Anthem, and you coach these guys the rest of the day."

He grinned.

"Bill, you know I'm from Brooklyn, right?"

I told him I knew.

Neil Diamond said, "I hope you beat the hell out of them."

Giants fans are everywhere.

But I felt the game we were about to play meant a little more to me than the rest of them. Because I'd come the farthest for it.

2

Jersey Guy

My first memories are of Jersey.

We'd lived in Pennsylvania and Illinois when I was a baby, but it's not anything that I remember too well. My father had worked for the FBI; that was after Georgetown and Georgetown Law. But he quit the day after I was born, and went to work for US Rubber. I think my mother had a lot to do with him leaving the FBI. She didn't much like knowing whether he was going to come home or not.

I work horrible hours as a coach, but at least Judy Parcells knows where her husband is.

My father's real name was O'Shea, but he was adopted by the sister of his real mother, who in turn married a man named Parcells. So my dad was Charles Parcells, known as Chubby to his friends. I didn't know until I was about twenty-two years old that he had been a track star and a football star, all-American at Georgetown in fact. I used to hear some "If you can be as good as your father was..." when I was growing up, but he never talked about his athletic career. My father's attitude went like this: Do it, don't talk about it. I'm like him that way. There were scrapbooks around when I was young, but he never opened them and when I did, he never paid much attention to them.

Chubby Parcells was humble about what he'd done in sports, and he wasn't going to push sports on me.

My mother, the former Ida Naclerio, was an Italian girl from Woodridge, which is even closer to Giants Stadium than Hasbrouck Heights. The house where she grew up is just up the hill from my Giants Stadium office, as a matter of fact.

I grew up a Giants football fan and a Red Sox baseball fan. My father was an obnoxious Yankee fan. And in my growing up years, he had a lot to be obnoxious about. The only team that could beat them at all in those years was the Red Sox. If you walk into my office today, you'll find a white golf shirt with the Red Sox emblem on the breast; on my desk, you'll find a paperback filled with trivia about the Sox. Ask me questions, I'll give you answers. When we beat the Redskins this past season on the Monday night game of October 27, the first thing I found out when we got back into the locker room was the final score of the seventh game of the World Series.

Mets 8, Red Sox 5.

It was a result I understood perfectly from my youth.

Baseball was my game growing up. I followed the Red Sox and I listened to Yankee, Giants, and Dodgers games on our Bendix radio. To this day, I know all the guys who played on any of those teams in the late '40s and early '50s. My father bought me my first bat and mitt when I was five years old. And right across from our house there was an empty lot that had been used for Army drills during World War II. It was bookended by Curtis Wright Aviation at one end and Bendix Aviation at the other. That was my first ballfield. That's where the games were played. And that was the place where I started to love sports.

The bigger I got, the more football began to take over. I was a Giants fan all the way. My favorite television program was "Marty Glickman's Quarterback Huddle" on channel 5, which at the time was the same station Jackie Gleason was on. Glickman used to have them all on: Charlie Conerly, Joe Scott, Arnie Weinmeister, Em Tunnell.

After we won the Super Bowl, the most emotional person at our party was Conerly, who'd been the quarterback when the Giants won in 1956. I didn't tell Chuckin' Charlie we had a bond that went back all the way to "Marty Glickman's Quarterback Huddle."

I went to my first Giants game at the Polo Grounds in 1954, saw them beat the Steelers. I was thirteen. After that, I'd get to see two or three games a year. I'd go with neighbors, or our Little League baseball team would go. It was that way until I went off to college. By the time I was in high school, we'd moved to Oradell, New Jersey, and even though we went to different schools, I used to play some playground football with Vince Lombardi, Jr. His father was one of the Giants assistant coaches then, and that made me root for them even harder. There were friends of mine who knew Vince Jr. a lot better than I did, and they got to go to games with him sometimes, which made me mad.

I wanted to go to those games.

By then, I was hooked. A neighbor of ours had season tickets, and he took me to the Giants–Browns playoff game in 1958, the snow game that Pat Summerall finally won with a forty-eight-yard field goal. The next week, the Giants played the Colts in the sudden death game. That one I couldn't go to. But I listened to it on the radio. I was out with a bunch of my high school buddies and some girls. We were at Lake Hopatcong, biggest fresh water lake in Jersey. Everybody goes ice skating except me.

Ice skating? What was that? The Giants were playing Johnny Unitas and Raymond Berry and Alan Ameche in the *championship* game. The rest of them skated. I sat for three hours in the car, listening to the game on the radio.

Ameche finally goes around right end in sudden death. Colts 23, Giants 17.

Devastation.

I met Mickey Corcoran when I was a sophomore in high school.

It was a new school, River Dell High, a regional school for Oradell and River Edge. The first year we played a junior varsity schedule, but we had the same coaches who'd be the varsity coaches when we got to be juniors and seniors. Mickey was the basketball coach. He was the same then as he is now: He was a student of all sports, not just basketball; he was demanding; and all he talked about was winning.

I've got another friend a lot like him in football: Al Davis of the Raiders. His philosophy is, "Just win, baby." Mickey's always thought the same way, except for the baby part.

He is a beauty. Next to my father, he's been the most important influence in my life. To this day, he is one of Bob Knight's closest friends too. When Indiana won the college basketball national championship last March, Mickey was in the stands at the Superdome in New Orleans, using one of Bob's tickets. With us winning and Indiana winning, he thought of it as a Mickey Corcoran parlay.

Way back in January, before we'd even won a playoff game, Mickey said to Knight, "Parcells is gonna win this SOB, and then you're going to win too."

It was a pretty good couple of months for Mickey, who watched us both grow up as coaches.

Mickey is sixty-five years old now. He's around our team all the time, and he knows it better than I do sometimes. Because he knows *athletes,* and he knows athletes as people. All Mickey wants to know is which players can do the most to help you win the game. I kid him sometimes about how rough Giants games are for him, what with him playing the game for players and coaching it for me. I talk a lot about being a Jersey guy. Mickey is the original: He's got a tough Irish face, he seems bigger than he really is, and he's always wearing a hat.

When Mickey got me at River Dell, I was already six-foot-two and 180 pounds, and I was one of the biggest kids in the school. And right away, I could see that this coach was different. It was always defense with Mickey. If we had a two hour and fifteen minute practice, we'd spend ninety minutes practicing defense.

"Ball, you, man," Mickey was always shouting. "Ball, you, man." On Mickey's team, it was an excellent idea to stay between your man and the ball, and contest the pass, and fight through picks. That's if you wanted to *stay* on Mickey's team.

We didn't have many great players. We didn't have many great shooters.

But we would go get the ball for Mickey Corcoran.

I didn't think of basketball as my sport. I liked it, and I liked football—even if I hated football practice—but I still thought of baseball as my sport. Even with that, I was drawn to Mickey. There was always something between us, even if he was throwing me out of the gym all the time.

I was a wise guy, and I was temperamental, and I had a bad temper (I still have these tendencies to be a wise guy, temperamental and have a bad temper, to tell the truth). Mickey didn't like that. My father didn't like that. What I didn't know at the time was that my father was in cahoots with Mickey to get me straightened out. My father and Mickey were a lot alike. My father challenged me to get good grades, telling me that I couldn't play sports if I didn't.

So he threatened to throw me out of sports if I didn't shape up academically.

And Mickey kept throwing me out of the gym when he didn't think I was shaping up athletically.

I'd wise off to him, or do something lazy, or kick the ball, and Mickey would just say, "Parcells, you're gone."

I played three years for Mickey, and a lot of what I learned from him in basketball has a marked influence on the way I coach football. From the time I was fourteen years old, Mickey talked about defense. He's *still* talking about defense. He thinks that defense is the only way to win in sports, and he's right.

Mickey says, "You play good defense and you're not going to win every game, but you're going to be *in* every game." He was right about that too. There were going to be days when the shots wouldn't fall, and there were going to be days when the other team couldn't miss no matter what you did, and sometimes the refs might get you. Those things you couldn't control. In Mickey's mind—and now mine—what you could control was your own defense, which at least gave you a chance. You could make sure you had a chance.

I didn't know all this at the time, of course. At the time, I was just a six-foot-two, 180 pound wise guy who did what he was told by Mickey Corcoran.

But his teachings were sinking in; retrospectively, I can see that. Mickey's big idea was that you should always have more ways to win than the other guy, at least going in. And defense was the hallmark of the big idea. Mickey said that if you could be better defensively, you could win if the sides were even offensively. All of a sudden, you had more ways to win just by working harder.

And we played man-to-man. Zone was a swear word when I was in high school. Zone? In Mickey's world, that was for sissies. It's that way in Bob Knight's world too. But he did play some zone this season at Indiana. And when he did, I nailed him.

Knight loves to make fun of the prevent defense in football. He especially likes to make fun of it when the Giants play it. "All that PRE-vent defense does," he'll say sarcastically, "is PRE-vent the Giants from winning."

So one night over the winter, I was watching the Indiana–Notre Dame game on cable. The next morning, I called Knight in Bloomington.

I said, "Coach, I watched the game last night. And Mickey and me were wondering: What exactly do you call that defense where you've got two guys out front, three guys in back, no pressure on the ball, and then they throw it down low to the big guy and he scores a layup?"

Knight was Knight.

"We call it the PRE-vent defense of college basketball," he said.

Mickey also taught me to be prepared for situations in a game, to see them coming, to be a step ahead. Some of my defensive guys now on the Giants—George Martin, Harry Carson—will tell me sometimes they're amazed that I can predict what's going to happen during games. It's no gift; it's preparation. It's all those eleven o'clock nights with the assistant coaches during the season. And it goes back to Mickey, and River Dell High. There'd be eight seconds left in the game, and Mickey would call time out, and diagram a play. Then he'd say to me, "I'm going to get you the ball here, with your back to the basket." Then he'd show me what the defense was going to do, and how this guy was going to slide and this guy was coming over to help out.

But I was supposed to score.

If he didn't think I could make the shot against the defense, he wouldn't have called the play.

Mickey's gift—one of them, anyway—was breaking things down in a hurry, giving you something to *rely* on, eliminating the surprises, giving you *enough* information without giving you too much. Mickey gave the facts; it was up to me to provide the response. He couldn't give me all the experiences he'd ever had with that back-to-the-basket play in that situation. He couldn't tell me what move to make. But during that time out, he would get me ready.

After the Super Bowl, I thought about the big fourth-and-one situation in the third quarter, and the way Jeff Rutledge handled it for me, and I decided it was pure Mickey.

It was early in the third quarter actually, still 10–9 Broncos. We had the ball on our forty-six-yard line. First it looked like we were in punt formation, then we shifted into a regular set, with Rutledge over center and punter Sean Landeta lined up at running back. And it was Rutledge's call as to whether he tried the quarterback sneak, or just went back to Plan A, the punt.

It was his option. He knew the called play was the sneak. If the Broncos stayed in their regular defense, and the inside linebackers didn't get up on the line and get into a down position, Jeff was supposed to go for it, roll the dice.

But if the Broncos went into their goal line defense, or if a big crowd suddenly developed in the middle with the linebackers coming up, he was supposed to step away, the ball was to be snapped to Landeta, and he was punting all the way.

Jeff let the thirty-second clock run down almost into delay-of-game. It looked to him like Denver was staying in its regular defense, thinking we were bluffing on the sneak, maybe getting ready to run some kind of trick play. But Rutledge didn't want them to move the linebackers up at the last second.

So he waited until the last second.

There he was, backup quarterback, standing there like the most relaxed person in the Rose Bowl, while the clock went eight...seven...six. We'd told him to wait as long as he possibly could. If he bent over center and started calling signals, then we were committed to going for it, and I've probably called a very bad play if Denver switches defenses.

I knew we'd set up the situation for him best we could, told him what to look for. We'd given him *enough* information.

But ultimately it was his call. Denver stayed in the regular defense, Jeff sneaked, got the yard, got the first down, we kept the ball. We scored a touchdown on that drive, and a field goal on the drive after that, and a touchdown on the drive after that, and all of a sudden it was 26–10 in Super Bowl XXI.

And I'm not sure how the game goes if 1) we punt on fourth-and-one from the 46 or 2) Jeff tries for the first down and doesn't make it.

That's why you run the play. It was like being back at River Dell, only I was Mickey and Jeff Rutledge was me, and he was getting the ball with his back to the basket, eight seconds left in the game.

What I mostly remember about high school was practicing. I mean, I cruised some. It was the late '50s, Jersey, cars were very important in your life. I had a '56 Ford. I'd earned the money for it in the summer; Chubby Parcells didn't give me a dime for it. And I paid the insurance. And when something went wrong with the car, the car sat in the driveway until I somehow earned the money to get it fixed. No gas money either.

Hackensack was where I cruised in it—Main Street in Hackensack. But not a lot. It seems like most of my life was spent practicing (it seems like most of my life *now* is spent practicing).

By the time I was a senior, football was my best sport, but there were still colleges interested in me for other sports. Seton Hall wanted me to play basketball, and so did Fordham. I think that was Mickey's doing, frankly. I think he knew somebody at those schools—or knew somebody who knew somebody—and that's where those offers came from. In those days, there weren't many baseball scholarships being offered, but a lot of people talked to me about playing baseball.

But football seemed to be the way to go. I'd played both ways, linebacker and tight end, and done pretty well at both. Auburn offered me a scholarship. So did Clemson. But thanks to my father, I'd done well enough in school so that the schools I became interested in were more academically oriented. I thought about some Ivy League schools, and ended up going to Colgate.

I played football and baseball at Colgate my freshman year. And I hated the place. I had become irresponsible in a lot of ways, and the problem was more me than Colgate: I liked playing there, I knew I *could* play there, but the attitude about sports was just different than what I expected. I didn't think I was better than everybody else, just different. I felt like I was looking around all the time and thinking the same thing, over and over:

These freaking guys don't want to win.

I was eighteen years old, so of course I knew everything.

Looking back, it's fairly safe to assume that there were guys in the baseball lineup, guys in that football huddle, who wanted to win as much as I did, more than I did. I just couldn't—or wouldn't—see it at the time.

I made it through my freshman year. I went back for my sophomore year, reluctantly. I practiced with the football team for two days and then I quit the team. And quit Colgate.

"What are your plans now?" my father asked.

I still had some wise guy in me.

I said, "Join the Marines."

Actually, I didn't have any idea what I was going to do. I knew my father and mother were upset with me. Mickey Corcoran was extremely irate when he found out. And I had no prospects.

My father laid it out for me.

He said, "You either go back to school somewhere this semester or I will never help you out financially with school ever again."

It worked out the way things like this usually work out for me: I had a friend somewhere. Somewhere turned out to be Wichita State. Mickey called out there and talked to one of the football coaches and said, "I've got this player who can play a little if you think you might want him." So Wichita State said it would give me books and tuition for a semester and give me a tryout in football.

Mickey told me all that.

It was the fall of 1961. I got into the car and drove to

Wichita. Other than one summer, I wouldn't be back to Jersey for a long time, until 1981, when I came back to work for Ray Perkins and the Giants.

And there was a lot I didn't know at the time. I didn't know it was going to be leaving home for good really. I didn't know I was going to meet my wife in Wichita.

I certainly didn't know that I was going to spend the rest of my life working at football in one job or another.

Wichita State. Hastings. West Point. Florida State. Vanderbilt. Texas Tech. Air Force.

Even Greyhound doesn't give you tours like that.

3   •

Parcells' Luck

Despite the fact that I wasn't a very good football player, I was drafted by the Detroit Lions out of Wichita State. I went to the Lions camp and got cut. I could make the whole experience a lot more dramatic than it was, but the fact is, I expected to get cut. When I did, it was the last in this string of lucky experiences at Wichita State, where they always thought I was funny:

1) I met Judy Goss, a secretary in the Sports Information office, and married her.

2) My roommate was Gene Dempsey, who remains one of my best friends today. Gene works now for the Drug Enforcement Agency in St. Louis. He's been with the DEA for eighteen years, and he's one of several people who've helped educate me

about drugs and drug users and the psychology of that world. To this day, when we play the St. Louis Cardinals, Gene and I have dinner the night before the game.

3) I had a taste of major college football. Wichita State had good teams in my years there, and seemed to be sending three or four guys to the pro's each year. Our quarterback, Hank Schichtle, ended up getting drafted by the Giants in 1964. One year we played in the Sun Bowl. Tulsa was a big rival at that time; I played against Jerry Rhome and Howard Twilley. Brig Owens, who went on to be a great defensive back for the Redskins, was the University of Cincinnati quarterback. Charley Taylor, a running back then, was one of the best players in the country at Arizona State. It was a brand of football I wasn't going to see at Colgate.

4) I decided I wanted to be a football coach somewhere down the road. I didn't know how to go about it. I didn't have any idea if you could break in right after college. But in my heart, I knew it's what I wanted to do. I liked the life. I'd *always* liked the life. I used to bitch about practice, but the truth is, I wouldn't have known what to do with myself without some kind of practice once school let out.

5) Dean Pryor, who'd been backfield coach at Wichita State, got the head coaching job at Hastings College. He got it the year I graduated. And he told me that if things didn't work out in the pro's, he wanted me to come help him coach at Hastings in the fall. He told me he couldn't offer me much money—the offer was $1000 for three months work—but that if I was as interested in

coaching as I'd told him I was, I had to start somewhere.

It turned out to be Hastings, an NAIA (National Association of Intercollegiate Athletics) school that played in the Nebraska College Conference. The Nebraska College Conference is not the Big 10. We played Colorado College; its star didn't go on to fame and glory in the National Football League, he went on to fame and glory at NFL Films. His name is Steve Sabol. And we played Colorado Mines and Doane College and Chadron State and Kearney State, which produced guard Randy Rasmussen for the New York Jets Super Bowl team of 1968–69.

By August, I was at Hastings of the Nebraska College Conference, in an area of Nebraska where the big events of the fall were the opening of the football season and the opening of the pheasant hunting season.

I loved it.

I was a coach.

4

•

Hastings

Our first daughter, Suzy, had already been born and the second, Dallas, was on the way. We lived underneath a dentist's office, a one-bedroom apartment. The rent was $62.50 a month. There were no windows in the apartment, just cinderblock walls. It was clean. You just couldn't see out. It was like living in a tomb. But it was less than a mile from school.

The best thing about it was that we could afford it.

The town had about 25,000 people at the time. One of the biggest businessmen in town was the father of Tom Osborne, now the Nebraska football coach. Tom's father owned a car-and-tractor dealership. I think it was a dead heat as to whether he sold more cars or tractors.

It was like contract labor, being a football coach at Hastings College in the mid-'60s. Everybody chipped in. No job was too small. Dr. Lynn Farrell was the athletic director and the basketball coach, but he helped out coaching football.

Me? I was literally learning football from the ground up, because in addition to working with the defense, I cut the grass, lined the field, even helped build the lockers. And when practice was over, I helped wash the uniforms. But I was *coaching*. I wasn't a graduate assistant. I was one of the four coaches at Hastings.

And it was in that first job that I learned firsthand something I'd only observed with Mickey: You can't tell players everything you know. I was trying to do that. I didn't know a hell of a lot, but what I did know, I decided I was going to tell everybody, every chance I got.

Wasn't working.

Football players forget things under pressure. The way basketball players do, and baseball players, and probably even bowlers.

It just happens. And if you're a coach, there isn't a damn thing you can do about it, no matter how much you've preached and taught and cajoled and even begged.

Example: Hastings was playing Nebraska Wesleyan. Our best player was Jack Giddings, a fullback. But like everybody else, he had to play both ways, so Giddings was also a safety on defense. And all week long before the game, Giddings—along with the rest of the defense—had been hearing about this big bootleg play Nebraska Wesleyan liked to run. Mostly they liked to run it because it was scoring one touchdown after another. The quarterback would bootleg, throw, they'd score. Every week.

Coach Parcells decided Nebraska Wesleyan wasn't going to bootleg Hastings.

The guy responsible for stopping the play was Giddings. He wasn't just a terrific player. He was a terrific kid: conscientious, hard worker, kept his mouth shut, did his job. A coach's dream. Well, sure enough the game comes and Nebraska Wesleyan gets down near our goal line. They run the bootleg. They score.

I didn't take it all that well.

All week we'd practiced stopping that play, probably more than we should have. We can't stop the play. When Giddings came off the field, I was all over his ass. Remember, I'm only twenty-three at the time. Giddings is twenty. I get right in his face anyway. How many goddam times do we have to practice something? What does it take for you to freaking learn? On and on, in front of everybody. He's the best player on the team, and I won't let it die.

Dean Pryor, the head coach, finally had enough.

"Leave the guy alone."

To me.

I said, "But coach, we worked on the damn play all week."

Dean Pryor said, "Well, you didn't work on it enough because they scored."

Case closed.

The sound you heard on the sideline of the Hastings–Nebraska Wesleyan game was my mouth slamming shut.

I've never forgotten that moment. I didn't forget it as an assistant coach, and I haven't forgotten it as a head coach. Lesson? You always better be prepared to honestly take part of the responsibility yourself. The kid was a *good* kid. He was trying to stop the pass. He was really doing everything I'd asked him to do, busting his ass. So maybe the one who hadn't busted his ass enough was *me*. I give Dean Pryor a lot of credit for getting the whole thing straightened out right there. As a coach, you've got to prepare the proper learning environment for a player. You can bombard him with all the information in the world, but if you present it badly, if you don't break it down the way Mickey used to break down that last-second play, then you're screwed.

And don't blame the player.

Wherever you are, Jack Giddings, you helped me out a hell of a lot.

Even if the bastards did score.

We had a good season at Hastings, finished 7–2. But the best thing about the season was not seven wins. I had coached. I had a season under my belt. Pryor had given me responsibility. I wasn't watching somebody else do it. I was doing it myself. It was a start. I wasn't Lombardi, but I knew a hell of a lot more about the business than when I went there.

I'd also made my cool three thousand bucks.

When the season ended, we packed everything we owned into a six-by-eight U-Haul trailer and drove back to Wichita, where Judy's family lived. I'm not sure at that point what my next move should be. I'm vaguely thinking about applying to law school. A couple of guys I'd played with were at law school, and I thought that if I mustered up enough of the energy that got me into Colgate in the first place, I could handle law school.

But, as usual, fate stepped in. If you don't think luck

means anything in life, you haven't been paying attention. There was a coaching change at Wichita State. A man named George Karras came in and took over, and offered me a job coaching the defensive line and doing some work with the linebackers. I took it. After one year at Hastings, it wasn't like people were bombarding me with offers.

I took the job.

It was an idea all tied up in good and bad. The good was that the opportunity came along when I needed the work. And it was the same Wichita State that I'd played for, which meant that the competition was a big step up from Hastings.

The bad was that it was the same Wichita State I'd played for. It was just too close to my college career. I hadn't put enough distance between me and college. I'd end up coaching for two seasons at Wichita State, and I never really felt comfortable. I would keep feeling uncomfortable, in fact, right up until the whole staff got fired after the 1966 season.

But Tom Cahill, who'd coached me in high school, was the Army coach by then. Tom Cahill was also a very good friend of Mickey Corcoran's. See what I mean about luck?

We packed up the U-Haul again and drove to West Point. It was there I would meet a lifelong friend, a basketball coach named Knight.

It was also there that I really began to learn how to coach. Everything up until then had just been the appetizers. West Point was the beginning of the main course.

5

Coach
Knight

I think Bob Knight and I hit it off because he liked football so much and I liked basketball so much. The first time we ever met at West Point I was playing ball with a couple of his assistant coaches during a lunch break.

We were the same age, but he was already head basketball coach, and you didn't have to know a hell of a lot about basketball or coaching to see that he was going places. But he loved football. A lot of his friends were assistant football coaches. You listen to him talk even now, and he'll talk about football coaches and how a lot of them have influenced him, from Colonel Red Blaik at Army to Vince Lombardi to Paul Brown. I'd want to talk about basketball with Knight, and he'd want to talk about football coaches.

Or generals.

He is my friend. I've seen all the things he's done on the court, from the tantrums to the national championships, but the private man I first met in 1967 at West Point is still the man I know. The thing people find hardest to understand about Knight is what great company he is. He is intelligent, he is quick, he is funny, he is loyal. He is sensitive as hell. We lived right around the corner from each other, and he used to come to our house after losses and hide; hell, we'd sit up all night and talk, go over every play of the game sometimes.

We both knew he was going to get a bigger job after Army, that ultimately he was going to outgrow that situation, go where he could recruit good players all the time. It was just a question of which one would be the right offer. While we were both at Army, he got offered the Wisconsin job and nearly took it. That one involved a couple of all-night conversations too. A couple of times he left the house and I thought he was going. He didn't.

You think the history of college basketball over the last seventeen years or so would be any different if he'd chosen Wisconsin?

I have a feeling it would have been a little different at Indiana, anyway.

During the basketball season, I loved just sitting in the gym and watching him take a team through practice. Could you tell with Knight? You could tell. Maybe it takes a coach to see it, I don't know. But it was just so obvious to me that he had greatness written all over him. There's so much theory involved in coaching, no matter what the sport. A lot of times you can just take out the word theory and replace it with the word bullshit. Coaches can talk themselves blue in the face. They can tell you this and that for hours, make themselves sound like Aristotle.

I want to see what's in front of me. I want to see it translated with what I see on the gym, and in the games.

What you're telling me, can I see the *evidence* once somebody blows the whistle and they start keeping score?

With Bob Knight, the answer was always, "Yes." His teams have always reflected what he was teaching them. He is a consummate teacher. Watch Knight on the bench during the game. For all his reputation as a shouter and screamer, hooter and howler, he really isn't up very much. He doesn't work the sidelines nearly as much as other coaches. That's because he's done his teaching in gym already.

Knight likes to say, "There's blackboard guys, and then there are coaches."

Don't wear either one of us out with b.s., is what he's saying.

"You listen to some guys talk," Knight says, "then you watch their teams play, and you wonder if the team is coached by the same guy."

I hear it all the time in the football world. If they do this, we're going to do that. But then if they do *that,* we're going to do such-and-such. Then you watch the game, and you want to call the coach up afterward and say, "And if they kick your ass, what do you do then?"

I used to scout for Knight. All I knew about basketball was what I'd learned playing for Mickey, but Knight would tell me exactly what to look for, and I'd get into the car and drive down and watch St. John's play somebody. Knight would have drawn up their offense, and then I'd try to see what the hell was going on.

But the most fun was to scout a game *with* Knight. Like Army would be playing in the National Invitation Tournament—it was when the NIT still meant something—and Knight would stick around after he'd played the first game of the doubleheader and scout the second game. One time it was Tennessee we were watching, and you have to understand that Knight knew the Tennessee offense and defense better than its coach did. For two hours, I just sat there and it was like I was next to this fountain of information that never stopped pumping. Knight would be there with his papers and his notes, and I just knew I was with one of the greats.

I used to say to Mickey, "He's winning twenty with the guys he's getting at Army. Wait until the sides are *even.*"

There's one thing that's never changed, from West Point to now: Every time I've ever watched a Knight team play, I've always thought they were going to win. *Always.* Every time he put his team on the floor, whether he had average talent or great talent, I always thought Knight was going to make it. I'm not sure I can pay anybody a better compliment than that.

This past March, when it looked bad for Indiana against LSU in the finals of the 1987 NCAA Midwest Regional, I was watching the game with Judy. Now she's always liked Bob an awful lot, for reasons that have nothing at all to do with coaching. She cares about him. She worries about him. When Bob threw the chair against Purdue, it upset her terribly. I saw it coming that day, by the way. I didn't know what was going to happen, but I could see something building up, and I knew when the explosion came, it wasn't going to be good.

It wasn't.

So now Indiana was down ten points, and it was getting late in the game, and Judy said, "I don't think we're going to make it."

I said, "Honey, I think you better go shopping." I told Knight the story later and he couldn't wait to share it with the world during one of his Final Four press conferences. The bastard got a big laugh with the story, or so I'm told. I don't think the press conference understood I was *serious*. My wife did. I was trying to get Indiana to the clubhouse with a win, and I didn't need negative vibes from my bride at that particular point in time.

Knight has always had tremendous respect for ones who've come before him in coaching, at least the ones who deserve it. It's rubbed off on me. I can remember one night when we were still at West Point, and the two of us drove up to the Catskills and had dinner with Clair Bee, the legendary coach who'd also written the wonderful Chip Hilton books for boys. And Knight, who's supposed to be the noisiest SOB in coaching, just sat there and listened to Bee for most of the evening, the way he would have with some storytelling grandfather.

Knight has always been like that, though. He wanted to meet top guns, men who understood what it was like at the summit. In basketball, it was Pete Newell and Henry Iba. But it wasn't just basketball. There were the football coaches I've mentioned. The only one he wanted to meet and didn't was Lombardi.

And Knight doesn't limit himself to coaches. Both Ted Williams and Johnny Bench have become great friends of his over the years. It's that type Knight's always been attracted to. Williams told him once that when he walked down the street he wanted people to say, "There goes the greatest hitter who ever lived." Knight says Williams is his number one sports hero, but I'm not sure whether it was because Williams was the greatest hitter who ever lived, or because Williams is one of the best fly fisherman in the United States. Knight doesn't make a big deal about it in public, but so is he.

But what Knight has done with people like Williams, I've tried to do in football. For instance, I have no more valuable friend in the game than Al Davis. And I'm luckier, and wiser, for it. Now I know Davis isn't one of the most popular men in pro football, and a lot of people don't care for him at all. To hell with them. Their loss. I happen to think Davis knows more about football than anybody around, and I'd be crazy to have access to the riches inside his head and not tap them.

It's not just Davis. I have tremendous admiration and affection for Chuck Knox, the Seattle coach who's also been a winner in Buffalo and Los Angeles. I don't think there's a man in the NFL who knows more about setting up a rushing offense than Chuck Knox. And there's Mike Holovak, the old Boston College all-American who coached the (then) Boston Patriots in the old AFL and is still in the league with the Oilers. These people are out there. The only thing that could prevent me or anyone else from learning from them is Mr. Ego.

Knight has become a tremendous Giants fan, of course. His team is my team. My team is his team. He loves Lawrence Taylor and Carl Banks. They're his two favorite players because they're probably the two best athletes on the team. I think one of his fantasies is Carl Banks playing in-your-jersey man-to-man defense for Knight at Indiana. Now that Daryl Thomas is graduating off the national championship team, I think he'd like to move Banks right in there at power forward.

Taylor went to North Carolina, which has a wonderful program in basketball. He's always telling me about Carolina and Dean Smith, and then I'm forced to remind him that when Indiana and North Carolina got together for the national championship game in 1981, it was my boy who came out on top.

Knight was on the sideline for one of the Giants-Eagles games this past season, and as he's walking through the locker room before the game, this voice says, "Hey Coach, you're not going to throw any chairs today, are you?"

It's Lawrence.

Knight wheels on him and says, "You don't worry about me today, you SOB. You just go out there and try to guard somebody."

Right then I knew they were going to get along fine. It was a sort of humor that Knight was used to hearing from me.

For a couple of years there, I used to like to call him up and tell him I was the Puerto Rican ambassador, and when could we expect him for dinner?

6 •

You're in
the Army Now

The year before I got to West Point, Tom
Cahill's team had gone 8–2. And when I
did get there at the age of twenty-five to
coach the defensive line, I could see why.
Cahill had put together a fabulous staff.
He knew football talent, and he knew
coaching talent. I was picking things up as
I went along, filing them away in the com-
puter, beginning to formulate my own
vague plan about things—deciding what a
head coach should be. And I learned the
importance of a crackerjack staff from
Tom Cahill, among other things. West
Point was my real basic training as a football coach.

Bill Meek, who coached the offense,
had been a head coach at Southern Methodist (may its football program now rest in
peace), Kansas State and Maryland. Dick
Lyon had coached at Ithaca College. John

MacAuley, who's still a friend of mine, had coached at Boston College. These men were older, first-rate, and generous from the first day with advice.

Looking back, the cast of characters on the freshman staff wasn't too shabby either. These were guys who'd been in ROTC programs in different schools around the country; they came to the Point with the rank of lieutenant, but the most important rank to them was coach.

And they could. Look it up:

—Bill Battle. He went on to coach Tennessee.

—John Mackovic. He went on to work with Tom Landry in Dallas, later became head coach of the Kansas City Chiefs. This past season, Mackovic took the Chiefs to the playoffs—they lost to the Jets at Giants Stadium—for the first time since the Nixon Administration.

And got fired by Chiefs owner Lamar Hunt.

Nice program they run in Kansas City. It makes you feel warm all over. Get into the playoffs, get fired.

—Al Groh. He became head coach at Wake Forest, and is with the Falcons now.

—Kenny Hatfield. When I stopped being head coach at Air Force, Kenny became head coach. He's at Arkansas now, doing an excellent job.

—Ray Handley. He's with me now, coaching the backfield for the Giants, and is simply one of the best in the business.

The freshman coaches became friends, because we were all about the same age. I hung around with them, and Knight. My fellow assistant coaches on the varsity became mentors. And Army became a fine experience for me. That's the best you can hope for, incidentally, when you're an assistant coach in college football—experiences. Stockpile them, sort out the important ones every once in a while. *Use* them. Because there are no great jobs. At least I've never had one. It is shit work, no matter how wonderful the head coach is, and the relationships you have with the other assistants. Maybe it's all right if you don't have ambitions to be a head coach someday; there are guys like that out there. But most of the guys in the job do want to be head coaches, so everybody is always looking around, looking ahead to the next job, plugged into that network of assistant coaches everywhere who somehow know who's going, who's staying, what's going to be opening up.

But you better keep learning. Hell, at West Point, I learned things from Knight that I could transfer to football, that I *still* transfer to football.

Knight never does drills just for the sake of drilling. It happens in sports all the time, and it is just a waste of time. Coaches love to drill. They drill because their coaches used to drill them. Clair Bee once gave Knight a note that he still has. It reads: "Clair Bee and Bob Knight do not believe repetition is gospel." Well, count me in on that. You don't have to do things a certain way because they've always been done a certain way. The notion that you do is just bullshit.

Every year at training camp, I probably pay more attention than the next guy to simple tackling drills. Sound silly? Maybe. But I've got this quaint notion that tackling is important to football, even if you've got Lawrence Taylor and Carl Banks and George Martin and Harry Carson and Leonard Marshall and Jim Burt on your side.

I make them tackle.

I don't want training camp to go too far without them getting a feel for the game again. They don't like the drills. I make them do them, because the drills have a purpose. Right away, they're not *watching* football. They're playing again. They're getting in tune. I'm not trying to teach LT to tackle. Or Burt. It goes back to creating the proper environment. Once you do, you get on to other things. But when they show up, they know every year that it's not going to be summer camp for big people. On other teams, I know guys think they can miss a training camp here and there.

Not many Giants ever miss a practice.

I stayed at West Point for three seasons. Then came the gypsy years, the blur years. Three at Florida State under Bill Peterson and then Larry Jones, and two at Vanderbilt under Steve Sloan, and then Sloan goes to Texas Tech and I go with him. I was like everybody else in the business, a transient, looking to hook on with the right coach in the right situation, get noticed, become one of those assistants whose name gets mentioned when a head job does open up.

And keep stockpiling those experiences, brother.

Florida State was my first experience living in the south, and it was my first experience with recruiting, and I didn't much like either. I turned thirty while I was at Florida State, and it was there I knew for sure that I was going to be a head coach someday, and I knew recruiting was going to be a part of it, and I just hated it. I hated the rap you had to give to high school kids, I hated the rap you had to give to their parents. I didn't cheat but I would have had to be blind not to see cheating go on at other schools, and I hated losing good prospects to the cheaters.

I liked Peterson. I got involved with strategy at Florida State, calling defenses, designing them. It was another small step up in responsibility. But there were times when this Jersey guy started to feel like one of those screaming, good-ole-boy southern assistant coaches. I didn't like the feeling.

I was getting caught up in the rat race, at a young age. I could feel the ambition growing. I felt like I was always looking around. Peterson left, Larry Jones came in. I met Dan Henning there, and he would become as close a friend as I've ever had in my life. Henning is one of the smartest, most decent people I've ever met, and one of the truly innovative offensive minds in the game. He's another one, like Mackovic, who got beat up by the profession this last season. He was coaching the Falcons, his fourth year there, and they got off fast, got hurt, still finished 7-8-1, and you could see Dan had things turned around finally and going in the right direction.

He got fired. He'll be working for Joe Gibbs in Washington this year, and eventually he'll be a head coach again in the NFL. In my mind, he's just a giant of a person, pardon the expression. When word got out that I was in trouble after the 1983 season—when I was sure George Young was out there courting old Schnellenberger—Henning was the first person to call.

"If it happens, you know you've got a job with me the next day as defensive coordinator," he said. It's merely a gesture I'll remember the rest of my life.

But at Florida State, neither Henning nor Parcells knew we'd ever be head coaches anywhere. You *never* know. There are no guarantees that you'll ever be in the right place at the right time. You play hunches. You follow this head coach to the next job, or you don't. Can he win there? Or is the next stop going to be the dead end?

You find yourself thinking, "Damn, if I could just get to Oklahoma, or Tennessee, or Southern Cal. That would have to be better than what I have."

But you're not quite sure.

And as you become a gypsy, your wife becomes a gypsy, and so do your children. By the time Judy and I got to Florida State, we had all three daughters. As it turned out, Suzy would get the worst of it, school-wise, and Dallas would get the next worst because they were the oldest. Jill has been lucky, because she ended up having seven straight years in New Jersey. Suzy went to school in upstate New York and Tallahassee, Florida, and Nashville, Tennessee and Lubbock, Texas (that hub of higher education). Then, finally, high school in Colorado. My transient life became her transient life. There was good news and bad news to that. I think she suffered academically because of the way I kept jumping from place to place every two or three years.

But I look at her—I look at *all* of them—and think the moving might have helped them develop faster as people, showed them how to adjust to different situations and environments and parts of the country. It's hard to intimidate my girls. They've always been able to walk in and do it. Acclimating became second nature to them. They didn't always like it. There were tears sometimes. They did it. It has been a wealth of experience for them.

Their dad was learning how to be a football coach. Hell, there's no great trick to that.

His daughters were learning to be tremendous young women.

In 1973, I took a job under Steve Sloan at Vanderbilt. Steve is an ex-Alabama quarterback who has now become athletic director there, but at that time he was the fair-haired boy of college coaching, young man on the go. Vanderbilt had been in the basement of the Southeastern Conference so long their fans had forgotten what sunlight looked like, but within two years Sloan had us in the Peach Bowl.

There are two gold medal things you can do in coaching, college or pro:

1) You can walk in and turn a program around, the way Steve Sloan did at Vanderbilt.

2) You can walk in, turn it around, and *keep* it turned around.

Folks, trust me on this: *2)* is a lot harder than *1)*.

At least I thought so. Because a couple of weeks after the Peach Bowl, Sloan was the new coach of the Texas Tech football team, and I had to decide whether I wanted to replace him at Vanderbilt.

I was thirty-four years old at the time.

They were extending the head coaching dream.

Okay, Parcells. Put up or shut up.

I shut up and went to Texas Tech with Sloan.

I just didn't think Vanderbilt was a good job. I

thought Sloan had made the smart play. He had come in at Vanderbilt, done an unbelievable job over a short period of time, then taken an upgrade, better deal. But when Sloan came to Vanderbilt, there was no place to go but up. I thought the only place for me to go was down. What Steve had done was a fluke, basically. I didn't think you could sustain a fluke.

I did have some funny conversations with myself while I tried to make up my mind:

"Okay, who you gonna beat?"

"Well, that's the question."

"You gonna beat Tennessee? You gonna go down the road with 90,000 people in the stands and beat the freaking *Volunteers*?"

"Nope."

"You gonna beat Alabama? You gonna go into Birmingham or Tuscaloosa and beat *Bear Bryant*?"

"Nope."

"LSU?"

"Nope."

"Georgia. Don't even bother answering that one, you know you're not going to beat Georgia, don't you?"

"Yeah, I know."

I went through the whole Southeastern Conference and I couldn't come up with one of the big teams I though I could beat consistently. The only team I figured I could beat consistently was William and Mary. Maybe Tennessee-Chattanooga. So now realistically I know I'd be taking a 3–8 job, a 4–7 job at best. If everything broke right, I might win seven games. Once. The way Steve Sloan already had.

I said no to Vanderbilt, yes to Sloan and Texas Tech.

The next thing I knew, I was in the middle of nowhere—Lubbock, Texas, is the state capitol of nowhere—watching the wind blow and wondering just where the next city was exactly.

Repeat: You're never really sure if the next job is a better job, even if you think it's a better job when you take it. Sloan found out. Three years later, he was out of Lubbock and on his way to the University of Mississippi.

And I was the head coach at the Air Force Academy. Was Air Force a better job than Vanderbilt? It wasn't, not really. But your priorities change. It was my first head coaching offer since Vanderbilt. I was thirty-seven now, not thirty-four.

I had made up my mind that the next offer I got, I was going to take.

7

Off We

Go...

Taking the Air Force job turned out to be
such a marvelous idea that within a year I
was out of football completely.

It only turned out to be upward mo-
bility because of the altitude in Colorado
Springs.

It turned out to be the Vanderbilt job,
only with future pilots.

Ben Martin was the coach before me,
and he was a lovely, stylish guy who'd come
to the end of his coaching career. And the
program was down. But when the people
from the Academy recruited me, I was told
they wanted to run a new, energetic kind of
program, the kind I'd been used to under
Cahill at Army.

So I showed up in Colorado, family in
tow, filled with the proverbial piss and vin-
egar. I felt like I knew a hell of a lot about
service academics after West Point. I felt I

was ready to be a head coach. I was already thinking about this being a stepping-stone to my coaching in the pros, because I was fully aware at that point that I was never going to be happy with the recruiting end of college football.

It took me only three months to know that I'd made a mistake. Again: All the things that were wrong with the Vanderbilt job were wrong with the Air Force job. Plus, I had an extra monkey on my back in the military.

Normally, any college athlete has to worry about two things: athletics and academics. I've never had a problem with that. I think they can handle both. Knight, who runs as clean a program as there is in this country at Indiana, has shown you can turn out good teams and good students. But at the military academies, you throw in the extra responsibilities of military training. So if you're going to have any chance at all to compete successfully, you've got to get some breaks from the higher-ups. If you can't get them to decrease the course loads slightly, at least *during* the season, you've got to sit there and watch your players go crazy with stress.

I had been promised a decrease in course loads during the season.

The promise was broken. And I could see what it did to the players. Some just stopped producing as the season went along. Some quit. A kid named Cormac Carney, wide receiver, had been one of the best freshmen in the country, and the next year, he had transferred to UCLA, because he just couldn't handle it all. And I could see a whole long line of Cormac Carneys, even if I was lucky enough to recruit players of his caliber.

I looked down the road and I knew Air Force was always going to be playing the Notre Dames of the world, and I knew there was no way the school could compete without a true change in philosophy (which seems to have developed in recent years). And I should have known going in they really weren't ready. I wanted to be a head coach *so damn bad* at that time, I had my eyes closed. I saw what I wanted to see, heard what I wanted to hear.

It is a very bad idea, no matter what your business.

All my athletic life, I'd believed in preparation. It went back to Dean Pryor and me and Giddings on the sideline of the Hastings-Nebraska Wesleyan game. Coach, we worked on it all week. Well, you didn't work on it enough, because they scored.

I thought I knew what I was getting into at Air Force, but I didn't. I hadn't prepared myself. We went 4–7 that season. We beat Texas-El Paso, Boston College (it was a long time before Doug Flutie, okay?), schools like that. In memory, it seems to me like the score was 41–39, either for us or against us, because getting into basketball games like that was the only chance we had to win.

We had a nice house. I was making more money ($10,000) than I'd ever made before. My wife loved the area and the house, my kids liked their schools.

And I feel like I'm trapped. I feel like it's going to take me four or five years to get the thing turned around. And even if I made the commitment, and Air Force had the commitment in me, I wasn't sure I could get it done by then. I was staring down the 4–7 road. Or the 3–8 road. Or the 2–9 road. Which is a dead end road. It was partly the fault of the people who hired me and partly my fault, but the bottom line was that I had finally become a head coach and I was just...goddam...miserable.

Pardon my French. But miserable by itself doesn't do the job.

And Ray Perkins called and offered me a job coaching linebackers for the Giants.

The Giants. From Giants Stadium, five minutes from Hasbrouck Heights. The Giants of the NFL. *The Giants* of Jersey.

I had just come back from a recruiting trip in California. I was proceeding with business as usual for my second season at Air Force. I didn't want to be there anymore, but I didn't have any options either. No Plan B. It was February. The phone rang.

Perkins.

The way he actually put it was this: "Would you be interested in flying east to talk about coming to work for the Giants?"

Was he kidding?

I would have walked.

I'd met Ray Perkins briefly when I was still at Texas Tech. He was working for the New England Patriots at the time, and he came to scout some players, and also to visit with Steve Sloan; they'd both played for Bear Bryant at Alabama, Steve as a quarterback, Ray as a split end. Steve introduced us. We didn't spend a lot of time together, but Parcells' luck was still working on full cylinders, because something about the meeting stuck.

Perkins is from Mississippi originally and I'm this guy from Hasbrouck Heights and Hackensack, and we're not too much alike as people or in background, but we're a lot alike in coaching. We both like to work hard, neither one of us is afraid of long hours, we don't act flamboyant in public but we're willing to take chances on the field. We say what we mean. Bullshit is not a big part of our makeups. We understood each other from the start. Perkins is a lot like Knight in this respect: What the public thinks it knows about him—and the press—is pretty far from the reality of the man. He's painted as being a robot, unfeeling, bloodless, whatever.

Now *that's* the kind of b.s. I'm talking about. Perkins is loyal and generous, and not just because it turned out he was so instrumental in my career not once, but twice. When we see each other now, it's like we just saw each other five minutes ago; it's that type of friendship.

He's also one of the top people in the business of coaching. College or pro. He started to show it with the Giants, and he showed it when he went back to Alabama. There was a lot of screaming when he left the Giants for Alabama, but those people never make a peep when a coach gets fired before the end of his contract; contracts are sacred, it seems to me, as long as your boss thinks they're sacred. When the time comes that they want to get rid of you, a contract is a dishrag. Alabama was just something Ray had to do. It was his school. It was his dream, the way coming home to Jersey and coaching the Giants was a dream to me. It wasn't like I carried it with me every day of my life. It wasn't even like I thought about it a lot. But when it was offered, I knew. It was that way when Alabama came calling on Ray to succeed Bear Bryant.

But I always knew he'd be back in the pros. I just thought everything about Ray—temperament, philosophy, personality, his own hatred for recruiting—made him better suited for the pros. We had a plane ride together after he left the Giants, and I said, "You'll be back in pro football in five years."

He said, well, he didn't know, he was going home, et cetera, et cetera.

Well, he's back with the Tampa Bay Buccaneers, and wait and see the job he does there with Vinny Testaverde and friends.

When he took the job, I called him and said, "I was off by a year."

Perk laughed at that. It had taken him four years instead of five.

But this was 1979, and he'd just been hired by George Young to coach the Giants. It came down to Ray and Dan Reeves (if you don't think coaching is a small world, then explain to me why the hell we all keep bumping into each other), but George knew Ray and had worked with him back with the Baltimore Colts, and Ray got the job.

I flew east, and checked into the Sheraton hotel in— you guessed it—Hasbrouck Heights. We talked about his plans for the Giants, and how he needed linebackers who could play the damn game because he wanted to switch the team from the 4-3 defense it had been playing forever to a 3-4, and about his dreams. We didn't talk about my dreams, and how they were wrapped up in the Giants and coming home to Jersey, but Perk was smart enough to know they were definitely in the room with us.

"So what do you think?" he said finally.

I said, "When do we start?"

We shook hands. I was a Giant.

Hot dog.

I called Judy, excited as hell. She wasn't too excited about the news, but I didn't pay that any heed. Shit, I was a *Giant*. This was great for *me*. I flew home and submitted my resignation at the Air Force Academy. Now this made big headlines in Colorado, because I'd only been there a year, but at the Academy they basically understand it's something I have to do.

They also ended up with my old friend Kenny Hatfield as coach, and he frankly did a better job there than I did.

By now, I'm noticing how cool Judy is to the whole idea. She doesn't like the east. Her only experience with living in the east had been when we were at West Point. She doesn't have a good impression of that whole area of the country. Her experience had mostly been the midwest, and those stops we'd made in the south. She's happy with our life in Colorado, she's made friends there, she's tired of moving.

And I keep telling her, "I can't *not* take this job. I've never had a pro offer, I don't know when I'm going to get another pro offer. Honey, you know how they talk about opportunity knocking? Well, in my case, it's about to kick in the damn door."

In *my* case.

I can't not take this job.

No question it was a terrific job offer for *me*.

Judy? Hell, just help her pack the bags and give her

a boarding pass, just like always. She'll go along. The girls too. Great sports, the girls. The economy's bad in Colorado? We might not be able to sell the house right away, and we're not exactly rolling in dough? No problem.

I was going to work for the Giants.

Judy kept saying, "I just don't know if I can move again."

I kept figuring she'd come around.

Just like always.

I left things up in the air and flew back east and checked back into the Sheraton, and went to work with Ray Perkins. The days were great, the nights were awful. The days were filled with talk about linebackers, and getting ready for the draft. The nights were spent on the phone, and I didn't exactly have to be a private detective to know that things weren't getting any better in Colorado. No spring thaw. The house wasn't getting sold, and my wife didn't seem all that upset about it.

It got worse every night. And little by little it got through my thick skull, even long distance, that I was going to have to make a choice between family and job. Judy wasn't going to come east; I don't think she ever had any intention of coming east. The girls were happily set up in their schools.

And I decided that they needed me more than Perkins needed me.

Sometimes somebody hands you your dream, and you've got to hand it right back. I walked into Perkins' office—the same office I have now—and explained everything to him, and resigned.

He said, "Listen, I'm sorry, but I understand. Do you think you can stay through the mini-camp for our veterans we've got coming up?"

I told him sure.

I stayed through the mini-camp, and through what I'd convinced myself were going to be my last days as a pro football coach. Hey, you hear about that guy Perkins hired from Air Force? Got cold feet after two months.

Pat Hodgson was the receivers coach for Perkins, just as he is now for me. Pat and I had worked together at Florida State. When the day came, I checked out of the Sheraton with what stuff I had, and Pat drove me to Newark Airport. I don't think either one of us spoke a word, other than Pat asking if I had my ticket. I thought, Yeah, ticket out of the business.

It was a Continental flight. I sat in coach.

And cried all the way back to Colorado.

8

.

Out of
My League

There was nothing heroic about it. I made
the proper decision, the same sort of decision husbands and fathers have to make all
the time. The fact that I was a football
coach giving up a big football job didn't
make me a candidate for the Nobel Prize.

I couldn't do what I wanted to do.

I did what I had to do.

My daughters would have cried some,
but they would have packed their bags. But
I figured I owed Judy one. A big one. She
had been on the same Greyhound, see-
America-the-hard-way tour I'd been on.
Wichita State. Hastings. Wichita State.
West Point. Florida State. Vanderbilt.
Texas Tech. Air Force. If you averaged it
out, it was a move every other year of our
marriage. Sell a house, buy a house, find
the new school, make friends.

Then say good-bye to friends, sell the

house, and get on to the next stop.

Knight says that a lot of coaches reach the point in their lives that I reached with the Giants offer, and don't have the guts to walk away the way I did. Knight says I was real smart to step back and see where the hell I was. I appreciate the sentiments, but I didn't think about guts, or being smart. Nobody whispered in my ear that it was all right, in eight years I'd be *head* coach of the Giants in Super Bowl XXI. Nobody told me that Perkins wouldn't forget me and my luck would hold and I'd get back in the game, no problem.

I thought I was out, but I felt what I was doing was necessary.

I also was not overloaded with prospects. I was thirty-eight-years-old, going on thirty-nine. I had one skill: football. I'd been working the skill for nearly fifteen years as a coach. I'd been running the treadmill real hard, but I didn't have a lot of money.

I think it's called a midlife crisis.

Now I'm a confident person. I've always been a confident person. I knew I could find something. But I still had house payments to make and a family to support. I figured that even if I didn't find work for six months, we could survive. After that, I didn't know what the hell we would do.

And the reality of it all didn't hit me until I got back in Colorado. Now understand: I had given up the Giants job, quit on Perkins, to alleviate a sense of urgency at home.

Then I got back home and realized that giving up the job had created another sense of urgency.

My wife said, "What in the world are we going to do for money?"

Beautiful. In the Giants press guide now, it says I resigned that first job with the Giants "for personal reasons to enter private business." It reads harmless. It's accurate too. The reasons *were* personal. And I did enter private business. It was just the one didn't follow the other right away.

I had met a lot of people as Air Force coach. I had made the connections you can make as a college football coach, you know, within the community. I started working the phones.

I was vaguely thinking about something in sales. Football coaches know a lot about selling: themselves, their program, their philosophy, their offense and defense.

I'd find a new area of selling.

I finally went to work for a company called Gates Land, subsidiary of Gates Rubber, a big tire-and-rubber outfit in Denver. Gates Land was developing about five thousand acres in an area, Cheyenne Mountain, adjacent to the Broadmoor Hotel. Situated on the five thousand acres was this wonderful place, The Country Club of Colorado; around it, Gates Land was building all sorts of residential and custom homes in various lush settings. I was actually still close to the Air Force Academy in Colorado Springs.

That was only if you measure in miles.

I was in the business world now.

In the morning, three mornings a week, I'd take a real estate course, learning enough to get a license to sell the land we were trying to sell in the afternoons. The course took seven weeks. I passed it with flying colors. Pin a gold star on the coach's forehead.

In addition to the real estate side, I was also acting as athletic director at the country club. They already had a tennis coach and a swimming coach and a general manager. I was more a coordinator than anything else, setting up independent programs that would combine, say, swimming and tennis, and what-not for the members and their children.

Are you following? I was Julie from "The Love Boat," only bigger.

I can't describe how much I hated it. Was real estate school interesting? Well, it was actually. It was something new and different, and I was pretty good at it, and at least I knew that I had one new skill other than football. But I was miserable. I'd turned into a damn yuppie, at the age of thirty-eight. And I knew that pretty soon a football season was going to start without me for the first time since junior high school.

Things were fine at home, though. For the first time in my life, I was having breakfast with the family. As a coach, I was used to being up and out of the house by six, five-thirty sometimes. (I'm the same way now with the Giants; the alarm goes off at five, and I'm up and moving.) Now I was playing Robert Young in "Father Knows Best" every morning. My wife thinks this is a fine idea. Plus I'm taking her out more, we're doing more things together than we ever have, we're taking rides up into the mountains, my weekends are free for the first time since we've been together.

It's all very nice, and it's what I knew it was going to be like, but I'm split. I am very happy things are going so well at home.

I was making $45,000 a year, a little more than I had at Air Force. And I was just *dying* inside.

May moved into June and June moved into July, and reading the sports page every morning was like getting knifed, because the football training camps had opened. Rookies were being waived, veterans were getting hurt, this guy or that guy had signed.

There were an awful lot of mornings when I started to dial Perkins' number and beg him to take me back, even though I knew he'd hired somebody to take my place.

I never made the call.

The irony of the football season, as I said, was that I was going to Denver Broncos games at Mile High Stadium, the same Broncos we'd play in Super Bowl XXI. My wife went to the games with me. We'd sit in the same seats every Sunday, like a perfect football couple. The seats were in the end zone, at the end of the stadium where the dressing rooms are, opposite side from the press box.

You could fill up that stadium right now, leave just those two seats open, and I could walk right to them without missing a beat. That's how indelibly those Sundays in 1979 are imprinted on my brain. It was pro football, and I wasn't in it. Coaches I knew would come in with other teams, and we'd have dinner the night before the game, and then they'd help coach the visiting team on Sunday and I'd tailgate with Judy then go sit in the end zone seats, dressing room end, opposite from the press box. And die a little more.

If Air Force was at home, we'd drive up to the Academy and watch them play. I wasn't too crazy about that idea. Every time I walked into the stadium, I felt conspicuous as hell. I'd coached there the previous season, left the job, gone to the Giants, left the Giants, left football, and now here I was going to Air Force games. Maybe somebody should have given me the Forgotten But Not Gone Award.

But I went to the games, because it was football.

Friday nights, I'd do the High School Game of the Week for a Denver radio station. The play-by-play man was Jeff Thomas, a prominent local sports announcer, and a sweetheart of a person. God bless him, he knew how much I missed football, and even this was a chance for me to keep my hand in.

I wasn't exactly John Madden or Pat Summerall, the guys I consider the best in the business. If pressed, I guess I'd describe my broadcasting style as blabbering idiot.

Which I was in danger of becoming if I didn't find a way to get back to coaching football. Even my wife saw through the smiles and the stiff upper lip and the rest of that bullshit.

One night in the fall we were sitting watching television and out of the blue she said, "This is beginning to drive me nuts."

What was that?

"You're driving me nuts," she said. "I think it's time you thought about getting back into football."

She knew, and I knew. You are what you are. You do what you do best. Going all the way back to River Dell High, my life had been built around the orderliness of sports, the schedules and rules and regulations of sports. There was practice and there were games, and then the practice getting ready for the next game. One season blended into the next the way one practice blended into another. I wasn't built for anything else. I wasn't built for breakfast with the family at eight-thirty. What was that? For my entire adult life I really had been gone for at least two hours by then. I was a coach. I could sell all the real estate in the world, and I was still going to be a coach. I didn't want my damn weekends free. I wanted them to be structured around a football game. I didn't want to sit in the stands. I'm glad I took the season off, I know I did the right thing for Judy and the girls at that time. I was there when they needed me. Maybe it was more important as a symbolic gesture.

It didn't change the fact that it hadn't been a day at the beach for me professionally. From the time Pat Hodgson had dropped me off at Newark Airport back in the spring, I had been waiting for Judy to suggest I get out of the house and back into football.

Halfway through a television show whose name I certainly don't remember, I got up and made a call to Ray Perkins I'd been wanting to make for a very long time.

Six months that seemed like six years.

I said, "I want to come back."

Ray said, "I figured you would sooner or later."

He told me the Giants were playing Kansas City on Sunday. I told him I knew that.

"You want to have breakfast?" he said.

I flew to Kansas City and had breakfast with Perkins Sunday morning before the Giants-Chiefs game. And it was just so...*great* to see him and to see some of the players walking through the lobby.

I didn't ask Perkins for a job with the Giants. I just basically told him, in an expanded version, what I told him on the telephone: I wanted to get back into pro football.

I wanted to come back to the Giants. I wanted to work for him. But I knew I'd left him in the lurch, whatever my reasons.

Ray said, "I don't have anything right now. And I'm not sure if I'll have anything after the season, but I might. We'll stay in touch, and if I hear anything about other teams, I'll let you know."

That was good enough for me. My prospects weren't any better than when I'd flown to Kansas City, but my mind was made up. My conversation with Ray was my way of making a commitment to get back into the game.

We put the house up for sale again. This time we sold it. It was December by then. We had to be out by January 10, and I don't have a coaching job—I don't have a *nibble*—but I'm relying on Parcells luck again.

It had always worked fairly well in the past.

Steve Sloan was still at Mississippi. I called him and told him the same thing I'd told Perkins—my sabbatical, or whatever you want to call it, was over. Steve told me he'd get back to me as soon as he could. And suddenly the word was out that I was looking for work. I don't know who Steve called, or who Ray Perkins might have called, but the old coaches' network was working as well as ever.

Rod Dowhower was head coach of Stanford at the time (he'd later be head coach of the Indianapolis Colts before Ron Meyer). Dowhower said, "I hear you're looking."

"You bet."

He flew to Colorado Springs, and we had a meeting. He wanted me to coach the defense. I just figured this was going to be the job. My friend Ray Handley—I went all the way back to West Point with him—was on Dowhower's staff. I flew to Palo Alto to see the campus and just fell in love with Stanford, the way everybody who sees Stanford falls in love with it; it's just the most beautiful college campus in the world. I'm going to be back in coaching, I know Judy and the girls are going to love the setting.

Dowhower and I agreed to agree.

The next day, while I was still in Palo Alto, Dowhower took a job as offensive coordinator with the Denver Broncos. Them again.

But when I got back to Colorado, there was a message to call Steve Sloan. Steve said he had a job for me at Mississippi if I wanted it. Wanted me to be *his* defensive coordinator.

I told Sloan that sounded very good, let me think about it.

While I was thinking about it, Perkins called. He said, no, he didn't have anything for me, but to call Ron Erhardt, head coach of the Patriots. Erhardt just had the job of linebacker coach open up.

I said to Perkins, "I've got this offer from Steve at Mississippi."

Perkins said, "Call Erhardt."

I said, "The Mississippi thing is solid, I still really haven't coached in the pros. I probably don't have a chance to get the New England thing."

"Call Erhardt."

This, to me, is the kind of friend, and man, Ray Perkins is. Again: whatever my reasons, I had stiffed him after taking the job. He'd only seen my work for a couple of months. The truth of the matter was that I didn't have any pro experience. And now he was obviously pushing me on New England, practically acting as my damn agent.

You think I'm ever going to forget Ray Perkins?

I called Erhardt, and set up a meeting in New England. This was after I'd called *Sloan* back and laid out the situation for him. And Steve—who's every bit the gentleman Perkins is, every bit the friend—says, "I'm not withdrawing my offer. It's here. You go to see what they have to say in New England."

"I probably don't have a chance," I said. "You'll probably be seeing me in Mississippi in a couple of days."

Sloan sounded like Perkins.

"You just fly up there and see."

Remember, we'd already sold the house at this point. We'd gotten an extension, so we didn't have to be out of the house until February 13th.

But it was February 10th.

The meter was running.

I flew to Boston, drove to Foxboro, where the Patriots' offices are located. I met with Erhardt, whom I liked right away. I thought the interview went well. He told me he had some other candidates to see. Said he'd get back to me.

I told him the meter was running, that I had to have an answer, that I couldn't hold up Steve Sloan at Mississippi, that I had to be out of my damn house in about twenty minutes.

Erhardt called me back later that day at my hotel.

"The job's yours if you want it," he said.

I told him yes. Then I called Steve, who was, of course, a sweetheart about the whole thing.

"Give 'em hell," he said. "You've always belonged in pro football anyway."

9

Giant Dream, Part II

We had a great year in Massachusetts. Ron Erhardt and I developed both a working relationship and a friendship that would eventually move to Giants Stadium after he got fired by the Patriots. He was head coach and I coached his linebackers, then I was head coach and he was my offensive coordinator, and it didn't alter the friendship one bit. Judy and the girls loved Massachusetts, all of New England really. And I got my first extended taste of pro football.

I loved it.

I loved the whole atmosphere, the attitude of the players and coaches, the conditions, the accommodations, the *game*. Long hours? Hell, the long hours had been working at The Country Club of Colorado and coordinating swimming programs.

The Patriots would finish 10–6 that

year, and I felt like Ron had the thing going in the right direction. I actually thought I might be with New England for a while.

Wrong.

Opportunity, in the form of Ray Perkins, decided to pay a second visit to my door. Now the job with the Giants was defensive coordinator. *Of the Giants.* The job was mine, he said, if I wanted it.

Yeah, you could say I wanted it. The Parcells' family made what might be its last move for a long time. The move was back to New Jersey. Finally. It was 1981. I'd headed off to Wichita State in 1960.

I didn't know Perkins would be gone at the end of the 1982 season, I didn't know George Young would single me out of the crowd to replace him, I didn't know then that it was going to be the longest hitch of my life, and the one that would make me one of the big guys in coaching (and I'm not just talking about weight here).

I just knew that I was home finally, working for the team whose history reached right back into my own. When I first started listening to the Giants on the Bendix radio, watched them on "Marty Glickman's Quarterback Huddle" on the same television station that had Jackie Gleason, the Giants *were* giants. They were great. They hadn't been great for a while. They had played in championship games after they beat the Bears in 1956, but they hadn't won any. In the middle '60s, at the time I was first starting out in my coaching career, they had hit a stretch of bad road that would last all the way to Ray Perkins. I wasn't a passionate follower of the team in those years because I was working my own gypsy trail, on that Greyhound tour. But if you followed football at all, you knew that coaches came and went with the Giants, and so did general managers.

When I showed up in 1981 to work for Perkins, the Giants had had eight losing seasons in a row. They'd won thirty-one games—total—in those seasons. Perk himself had gone 6–10 and 4–12.

They were a long way from Super Bowl XXI. They hadn't made the playoffs since 1963. I didn't exactly come into the situation breathless, because I had left a pretty good situation in New England, or so I thought at the time.

But the Giants were still my team.

Perk said, "Build me a linebacking corps that I can build a defense on."

It was a defense that had ranked No. 25 in the National Football League the previous season. The only spot below it was No. 26. And it was a defense that had allowed 425 points.

I said to Perk, "It won't be easy."

It would turn out that I had some pretty good players to start with on that defense.

There was also this rookie linebacker out of North Carolina named Taylor.

10

LT and Harry
and the Playoffs

LT.

No. 56 in your program, No. 1 in the hearts of George Young (who drafted him) and Ray Perkins (who sure needed him or somebody like him after 425 points against and that No. 25 ranking in defense) and me, the guy trying to build a defense that might keep Perkins and me and everybody else on the staff around for a couple of more seasons.

LT was the Giants top draft choice in 1981 and the second pick in the draft overall, behind George Rogers, who'd won the Heisman Trophy at South Carolina and went to the New Orleans Saints (nothing against George, but when he and Lawrence were drafted, neither the Saints nor the Giants had been to the playoffs since the AFL-NFL merger. Well, the Saints still haven't gone, and the Giants have now been to the playoffs four times in the 1980s, won the NFC East once, the NFC and Super Bowl XXI. It was a fairly good pick, is all I'm saying). Lawrence Taylor had been an all-American at North Carolina, the Atlantic Coast Conference Player-of-the Year, and an ACC defensive legend. His senior year, one-third of his tackles were behind the line of scrimmage.

One-third.

You can look all that stuff up.

None of us needed his bio at the Giants training camp at Pleasantville, New York, summer of 1981. It was just right there to see. Now understand: I had some damn good linebackers waiting for me with the Giants. Veterans like Brad Van Pelt and Harry Carson and Brian Kelley. I had a rookie named Byron Hunt out of Southern Methodist who I figured was going to fit right in with them at some point and become a star.

But right away you could see Lawrence was different. Some athletes are. That one summer, Dwight Gooden went from being Gooden to *Doctor K.* You know? There is just something that certain athletes have that puts them a cut above, makes them special. Lawrence was *LT,* just about from the start. He had things to learn. He was raw as hell. His talent had carried him to us, and his No. 1 status and all that, and now he was going to have to use his head more than he ever did.

(It's interesting to look back now and see that both Gooden and Lawrence ended up in drug rehabilitation within a year of each other. Because they were both so special, the two biggest stars in the New York sport spectrum, young, seeming to have it all: talent, money, fame, bodies you figured would never betray them. It just shows you how cocaine works on your freaking brain, and doesn't care who the hell you are. I'll talk more about drugs later on, but other athletes ought to look at Gooden and Taylor and understand it could happen to anyone. They won't, of course. They all think they're Superman or something.)

First impressions of LT at Pleasantville?

Talented.

Extremely goddam talented.

Aggressive as hell.

Unbelievable quickness.

Great natural strength.

Hated to lose. You could see that right away. The whole notion of losing was like somebody wanted to stab him in the ear drum.

I liked him *very* much. So did Ray. After about five days of scrimmaging, he came up to me smiling one day after practice. Now Ray smiling after practice is total jubilation for anyone else.

"I came to camp wondering if he was everything he was cracked up to be," Ray said.

I knew he was talking about Lawrence.

I said, "So?"

Ray said, "Well, he's everything he's cracked up to be."

I laughed. "No shit." In our first scrimmage, all he'd done was sack the quarterbacks four or five times.

Now Lawrence didn't have a clue about a lot of things. He didn't know a thing about pass defense, or coverages. But he was willing to learn. More importantly, he was willing to listen. He's never been anybody you couldn't talk to because he already figured he knew everything. He was arrogant as hell on the football field, but not off it. I spent a lot of time with him—shit, I didn't have to be a genius to know that he was going to be the horse and me the world's biggest jockey—and he shut up and paid attention. Lawrence had been so damn good at Carolina that I think he was used to intimidating people. I made it clear from the start that intimidating me was just out of the question, and we've gotten along fine ever since.

My basic position with him has always been, "I'm going to say what's on my mind. I won't b.s. you, don't you try to b.s. me."

It's been that way in football, in the locker room, before he went into rehab, after he came out, when we weren't winning the Super Bowl and when we did. I've got forty or fifty other guys to worry about, I can't waste time making up lies for these guys. Lawrence knew from the get-go he could count on me to tell him the truth.

At least as I saw it.

It wasn't like I was taking him out to dinner every night in training camp, holding his hand. But there were individual meetings after the team meetings, there was a lot of one-on-one. Not just with me and Lawrence. Van Pelt talked to him and Harry talked to him and so did Brian Kelley. They didn't preach; they were going from the 4-3 to the 3-4 and they had a lot to learn too. And they all liked the kid, because even though he was a thoroughbred, they could see he was a worker too. He took all his natural confidence right from the start and used it in the classroom as well as the field.

On the field, of course, he was just running around everybody and jumping over them and scaring the hell out of our quarterbacks every day in practice. I came into training camp thinking I could ease him into the lineup slowly, along with Byron Hunt, give them bigger and bigger chunks of playing time, maybe have them playing regularly by the middle of the season.

It took me about three days to realize I could take that idea to the dump.

When Ray and I had our little chat at the end of the first week, I said, "Uh, I gotta get this kid into the *game.*"

Ray just gave me one of those long Perkins' stares and nodded, just like I'd told him the ocean was real deep, something obvious like that.

Lawrence was the start. He was the start of everything. George Young came in and gave the organization *organization* and Ray Perkins got through the hard times of 6–10 and 4–12 and drafted Phil Simms and got the Giants into the playoffs before he left for Alabama. I came along and eventually survived my own hard times and became, as it turned out, the right coach for this team as it was made up in the middle of the 1980s. Phil survived *his* hard times. Harry Carson and George Martin became the sort of veteran leadership every coach in this world dreams about. Joe Morris became the running back the Giants had never really had.

Everybody's sung in the chorus.

But if you look back, things began to turn around when Lawrence Taylor showed up at Pleasantville. It didn't hurt that I showed up along with him to coach him and the defense, frankly. We came riding in to clean up the town, couple of guys from an old western.

This isn't to take anything away from Ray, or a lot of

the other guys on the defense. But they'd been there the year before. Taylor hadn't. Neither had Parcells.

LT had 9–$^1/_2$ sacks his rookie season and 94 solo tackles and he assisted on 39 others.

You can look all that stuff up too.

But what he really did was change the way other teams looked at the Giants defense. He scared them, is what he did. He made them make changes. By the end of the 1981 season, coaches were drawing up game plans *around* Lawrence. Their top priority was dealing with this No. 56 who just seemed to be everywhere, whether they were trying to run the ball or trying to pass the ball.

And the Giants got into the playoffs again.

Relatively speaking, 1981 was a pretty good year for me. And LT.

Giants fans seemed to like it too.

It was like putting a puzzle together.

I took a rookie from Pittsburgh named Bill Neill, and put him at nose tackle in the new 3-4. I backed him up at nose with a free agent rookie out of Miami named Jim Burt, a guy who would do so much over the next several seasons to define the personality of this Giants team. We've got stars. We've always had stars. Simms is a star and Lawrence and Joe Morris and now Banks and Mark Bavaro. But it is guys like Burt, pluggers who made themselves into something, who have helped shape an attitude that finally made us champions. And it's an attitude that belongs to everybody now. Simms is a star quarterback who has the personality of an offensive lineman. He works as hard in the weight room as anybody.

I really think a lot of it comes from the Jim Burts, and all my other lunchpail guys.

Burt just came out of nowhere in that training camp of '81, became a wild man on the special teams, and earned himself a spot in my new defense. There were a lot of roads to Super Bowl XXI; Burt's was filled with potholes and the man just didn't care.

So I had two kids on the nose. Curtis McGriff, who had been on the nose, was moved to defensive end. Phil Tabor was another defensive end. He was around the Giants for a while and he was never a great player, but he was the type you wanted to have on your team. He's out of football now, but he's one of the guys I wished I could have had on the sideline at the Rose Bowl. And I had Gary Jeter and George Martin at the ends. Jeter I was never too crazy about. Just didn't like his work habits. Just wasn't my kind of player.

George Martin I was crazy about from the start. He is one of the gentlemen of pro football, of pro sports, and certainly of Giants history. He'd been a football and basketball player at Oregon, he was a terrific athlete, he'd been on losing teams at Oregon and then throughout his Giants career, and all George Martin ever wanted to do was win. There was some talk after we won the Super Bowl that George might retire. Well, I wasn't going to let that happen. I would have bribed George Martin to get him to come back for the 1987 season. Hell, I would have *blackmailed* George Martin to get him to come back.

I don't want to even think about what it's going to be like when Martin doesn't play for me.

He's a hell of a lot more than the guy who made the two big defensive plays in the two games we played against the Broncos last season. (In the regular season game, he fought off a blocker, leaped up, tipped an Elway pass, caught it, ran down the sideline with Lawrence as company, faked a pitch to Lawrence, fought off Elway—who's not a bad little athlete, by the way—with a *straight arm,* and scored our only touchdown of the game. It was only the best defensive play I've probably ever seen from start to finish. In the Super Bowl, of course, he nailed Elway for a safety.) George is a leader, with black players, with white players, with everybody. A coach can't be in the locker room all the time, and he can't manage the locker room all the time. And he can't know who's bitching and who's not. I don't have to worry about a lot of that because I've got George Martin down there. He just handles a lot of it. He does as much as me when it comes to letting the new guys know just how you're supposed to act and how you're supposed to work if you want to stay a Giant.

There's no one I've met in football—hell, in life—I respect more than George Martin. I couldn't have made it without him.

But it was Lawrence and the rest of the linebackers who became the heart of the defense. That's the way it's supposed to be in the 3-4. If there's one thing the 3-4 defense has done, it's made stars out of the linebackers. The 3-4 makes them take on more responsibilities than linebackers ever had in the past. They have to rush the quarterback like defensive ends, they have to plug the run like tackles, they have to cover the pass defense like they're defensive backs. It has become the position in football that attracts the best athletes.

Attracts the Taylors.

And the Carl Bankses.

In the old days, linebackers didn't have to be the size they are today, and they didn't have to have the strength. Look at those old Dallas Cowboys teams. They could get away with smallish guys like Chuck Howley and Leroy Jordan and D.D. Lewis at linebacker. Their main job was to help out a little on the run, and react to the pass, and let monsters like Bob Lilly do the dirty work and kill the quarterback.

But the game evolved, as games do, and more college coaches came into the pros, and they put more emphasis on the run, and so finally the 3-4 was born, and the linebackers were asked to do more of everything. Instead of reacting, they became attackers. hell, they became assassins like Lawrence Taylor. Faster than a speeding bullet. And, pal, more powerful than a locomotive.

I had a couple of guys to put in there. I had Taylor. I had Hunt, who'd pick up Van Pelt after he went down with a groin injury near the end of the regular season and play the outside like a veteran the rest of the way.

Van Pelt and Kelley had both had great Giants careers since they'd both showed up in 1973. The most games the team had won in a season—in their career up to then—was six. But they played hard every Sunday, no matter what the score, both of them on the outside, flanking Harry Carson. Van Pelt was never the most dedicated practice player of all time, but he never came up a quart low on a Sunday that I knew about. Kelley's out of football now. Van Pelt went from the Giants to the Raiders and from the Raiders to the Browns, and I was happy he got to be a part of a championship game finally, when the Browns lost to the Broncos. It would have been ironic as hell if Brad had finally made the Super Bowl, and found himself on the other side of the line from the Giants.

So Lawrence was on the outside. Hunt and Van Pelt sharing the season on the outside. I moved Kelley inside to play with Harry Carson, who is merely one of the all-time greats in the NFL at the position of linebacker.

All-time great?

Carson?

You're damn right.

He played on bad teams too. He was overshadowed at the start of his career by Van Pelt, who was sort of a fair-haired boy with the Giants, big blond guy out of Michigan State. And then LT showed up and looked like an instant immortal his rookie season and became the talk of the sport.

And all Harry Carson does is go out every year and get named all-NFL and gets named to the Pro Bowl. Eight times all-NFL for Harry Carson. Eight times to the Pro Bowl. I don't know how many guys in the history of the damn league have ever done that, but I'd bet a lot of money not many. People have this one image of Harry: a quiet, sensitive, well-spoken old Giant who'd put in his time in the losing years, and stuck around long enough to reap the harvest of the Super Bowl.

Well, they're right about that.

It's just that he isn't thought of often enough as an all-time great, which is exactly what he is. He'll turn thirty-four years old this season. He hasn't lost an awful lot that I can see.

I spent a lot of time with Harry Carson in 1981, because of the linebackers—he had to make the biggest adjustment, from a straight middle linebacker to one of the two inside guys in the 3-4. So we talked a lot about fundamentals and position and philosophy. And it's where I began to have respect for him. Because everything I asked him to do, Harry did. Now understand: He'd been in the league a while. He'd been all-NFL and he'd been to the Pro Bowl. He knew what he was doing, and he could have decided that he knew a shitload more about NFL defense than some guy whose whole portfolio was a year coaching the linebackers with the New England Patriots.

Harry didn't play it that way.

He listened like he was a rookie. And sometimes the things I told him weren't exactly music.

One time I said, "I think you've got an awful lot of talent and you've got good instincts and you're very *visible* out there, but I'm not sure you're a good linebacker."

Harry looked at me, very serious. He's got a great face, Harry. Some of the writers have said he'd make a good Othello. But you'd have to ask the writers, they're such big experts on Shakespeare.

And football.

And everything else, of course.

Anyway, Harry said, "What do you mean?"

I said, "You rely too much on your instincts, and good as they are, they're not enough to make you one of the best in the game, which is what you should be. Not because some player vote says you should go to the Pro Bowl. But because you really are."

Harry said, "You just tell me where we start."

They weren't any big things. I'm not trying to make myself out to be a genius or the savior of Harry Carson's career. But he'd fallen into some bad habits in regard to positioning and technique, and we helped get him straightened out. Mostly, he got himself straightened out, and eased right into the new defense. And the things he worked on in 1981 have carried him through to today, in my opinion, and they've put his career on a whole new plane. Year in and year out, he's become probably my most consistent player. I don't have to waste a lot of time talking to Harry, because he's gotten to the point where he just *knows*. Maybe two or three times a season I'll mention a technique thing to Harry, and that will be all, I just forget about it, because I know it's done.

What I'm saying is, I never did lack for weapons at linebacker. Just about every game since I've been with the Giants, I've been able to put two of the greatest ever to play the game out there, one inside, one outside. Harry and LT.

Later on, I got Banks.

You'd be amazed at how intelligent and brilliant and wonderful and all that other shit they've made me.

So that first year, we went 9–7.

We got the defense turned around. It just kept getting a little better every week, to the point where at the end of the regular season, I felt that if the sides were even offensively, we were going to win because of the defense. Mickey loved it. He'd been telling me all about it since I was fourteen. The last five games of the regular season, we gave up ten points, ten points, seven, ten and ten. Van Pelt went down, Hunt stepped in, didn't make a damn bit of difference. We were stopping everybody.

We made the playoffs, and that was all terrific.

But the best part of all came in the playoffs, because we beat the Eagles.

And that was one of the biggest things we did in 1981. As a coach, you have to set goals, whether you vocalize them all with the team or not. And I was obsessed that year with beating the Eagles. All the rivalries in the NFC East seem like big ones, full of tradition and all that stuff. You've got Giants-Cowboys, Giants-Redskins, Giants-Eagles, Redskins-Cowboys, Cowboys-Cardinals. It's a rough crowd. But the most important one for me was Giants against the Eagles, because the Eagles had been to the Super Bowl the year before. It's not like I was dismissing the Cowboys or the Redskins or anything like that.

I just felt we had to knock off the Eagles first, because they came into the season as a Super Bowl team.

How do we stop Wilbert Montgomery? He was in his prime then, a running back as tough as anybody in the league who could beat you inside or outside and carry the ball all day long. Our guys called him Timex, because he could take a licking and keep on ticking.

And how do we stop Ron Jaworski, the quarterback? And Harold Carmichael, the basketball forward they had at wide receiver?

We got the Eagles. We beat them in Philadelphia near the end of the regular season, then we beat them in the wildcard game. *In* Philadelphia again. Rob Carpenter had a big day, seemed to carry the ball every down in the second half. The defense held off the Eagles. We went to San Francisco the next week and lost. But we played the 49ers as tough as anyone did in the playoffs; if we'd gotten a few breaks early, we might even had won.

But nobody walked out of the season head down. We had a team now, you could see it. You could feel it. We had Lawrence, we had a defense, and I figured the defense could only get better. We won a playoff game, gave the eventual Super Bowl champs all they wanted on their field.

I knew I could pull my load in the NFL.

And we'd taken care of the damn Eagles.

11

Twelfth
Head Coach
in the History
of the Giants

George Young said, "With Ray leaving suddenly like this, I think the most important thing for the organization now is continuity."

December, 1982. December 15, to be exact. We were sitting in Young's office at Giants Stadium. He is a big man, big, round, balding man, with a soft, high-pitched voice. I was pretty sure he was about to offer me the job as head coach of the Giants.

I told him I thought continuity was important too.

George said, "You must know how impressed we all are around here with the way you got the defense turned around."

"Thank you," I said.

Of course, I'm thinking: hell, get *on* with it.

George likes to work at his own pace.

Always has, always will. Whether he's offering you a job, trying to replace you, or taking his time getting the last details worked out on your new, post-Super Bowl contract, George is usually George.

You can't goose him.

Finally he said, "Do you want the job?"

"Yes."

When the man offers you the one job you always wanted, I don't think you say, "Can I get back to you on it?"

A very strange year ended with me raking in the pot. Three years from picking up the phone and calling Ray Perkins and telling him I wanted to get back into football, he was on his way to Alabama to replace Bear Bryant and I was replacing him.

The 1982 season had been a mess from the start. Phil Simms got hurt again in the preseason. Back then, Phil was always getting hurt. He had been on his way to his best season—up until then—in 1981 until he separated his shoulder. Scott Brunner came in and took the team the rest of the way into the playoffs, quarterbacked the win over the Eagles and the loss to the 49ers.

In the 1982 preseason, Simms went down with a knee injury in the Jets-Giants game and that was it, he was out for the whole season, so Brunner became the man again.

It was more than just Simms.

Rob Carpenter held out into the regular season, into the players strike that followed, as a matter of fact. Carpenter had come over from the Oilers the previous season, and he'd really become the team's offense down the stretch. In that playoff game against the Eagles, it really did seem like Brunner stuck the ball in his belly every down the second half of the game. There was no question he had been a stud.

And it had happened in New York—the football is played in New Jersey, but all that silly star stuff happens across the Hudson River—so now he was a star, and he wanted to be paid like Walter Payton.

So when we started, Simms was gone and Carpenter was gone.

Lawrence got hurt, and he would have missed a lot of time except the strike came after the second game of the season.

Yeah, it was the strike year. The Players Association and the owners couldn't agree to a new collective bargaining agreement (the contract is up again, by the way, and a lot of people are figuring the strike of 1982 is going to be repeated during the 1987 season. Well, that's just terrific), and finally the players walked in September and didn't come back until November.

So it was like this with our guys at the start of 1982, summing up:

No Simms.

No Carpenter.

No Taylor.

No wins after two weeks of the season (losses to Atlanta at home, then Green Bay at home on a Monday night).

Then no season.

It was like all strikes. Nobody knew when it was going to end. There were always rumors, all you had to do was watch the news at six and eleven. A settlement was either around the corner, or maybe it wasn't. It was going to be a long one. Or a short one.

Nobody knew shit.

But if a settlement did come some Monday, or Tuesday, or Wednesday, the coaches had to be ready. So what we went through all the weeks of the strike was this weird sort of business-as-usual routine at Giants Stadium.

We kept drawing up game plans according to what the schedule was supposed to be.

Me and Bill Belichick and Romeo Crennel and Lamar Leachman and the rest of the defensive coaches would start work every Monday on our game plan. If the schedule said St. Louis, we got ready to look at St. Louis, looked at some St. Louis film.

Dallas?

Same deal.

We were having a normal week in an abnormal situation. Monday and Tuesday are the coaches' days anyway; practice doesn't start in earnest until Wednesday afternoon. So we'd meet all day Monday, and then we'd meet Tuesday and we'd put this plan together for this game we probably weren't going to play.

By Wednesday, we'd be ready for Dallas or St. Louis or whoever we were supposed to be playing next.

Then, starting Wednesday, we'd wait. We'd wait the rest of the week and then by Friday we'd know that even if the strike ended we weren't going to have a game Sunday. So we'd spend the weekends with our families, then

Monday we'd sit down and start drawing up a phantom game plan.

I've spent some strange times in football, but the strangest were those strike weeks at Giants Stadium, working on those game plans we never used.

It was like being defensive coordinator in "The Twilight Zone."

Lawrence got better during the strike and Carpenter finally signed. The season resumed with a game against the Redskins. This was the season the Redskins won the Super Bowl. The score was 27–17 for them, but they beat us worse than that. Then we went to Detroit for the Thanksgiving game and beat the Lions because Lawrence made a great interception and scored with it.

But nothing was ever in sync that year after the strike. We finally got back to a 3–3 record. Then we played a great defensive game at RFK Stadium but lost 15–14 when Mark Moseley kicked a field goal.

Then we lost to the Cardinals by a field goal. We scraped by the Eagles the last game of the regular season to finish 4–5, but missed the playoffs by a game.

That's the bad news.

The good news—for me—came with three games left in the season. It was then that Ray Perkins called us all together and told us he was leaving the Giants at the end of the season to go to Alabama.

Now you have to understand: I wasn't sure it was good news for me at the time. Sure, I thought I might get the chance to replace him if George Young decided to stay within the organization. After the way things had gone with the defense, I felt I was the logical choice on the staff. I thought. I felt. But if it didn't break that way, then there was also the chance that I might be on the street. A coach leaving, a coach getting fired—it just throws everybody into turmoil. If you're an assistant coach, you don't know what the hell is going to happen.

We didn't even know if Ray was going to be allowed to complete the season. Sometimes management just wants the guy to disappear, get on with things right away.

Anyway, Ray called us together and said, "I wanted to be the one to tell you I've taken the coach's job at Alabama."

He talked a little about that, then he dropped the other shoe.

"I think one of you guys might be offered the job."

Okay. So he was verifying what we all were thinking. I wanted to think he was talking about me, but there was no evidence.

But it didn't take long for me to find out I was the boy. The morning of Ray's press conference, George called me into his office, we had the continuity chat, he offered me the job, I took it.

In his office that day I said, "There's going to be a few guys on the staff I don't want to retain."

"That's completely up to you, you're the coach now," he said. "Just let's talk about any moves you make before you actually make them."

"Fine."

We shook hands.

I thought, this it is. Merry Christmas to me.

I was ready to go, but looking back, George Young did a smart thing by having Ray finish out the season, even if he did fall into lame-duck status. One, we still had a chance to make the playoffs; as it turned out, all we would have had to do is win either one of those games against the Redskins or the Cardinals, the two we lost by a total of four points.

Two, Ray finishing things out insured that I wasn't going to be judged initially by three games at the end of a strike season. It was not a comfortable time around the Giants. The team was shocked. Hell, here was the coach who'd put the team back into the playoffs for the first time in nearly twenty years.

Ray and I had a funny conversation on the team plane taking us to the St. Louis game. Because I wanted to ask him a thousand questions about the organization. And Ray wanted to ask *me* a thousand questions about college football, because I'd been in it for fifteen years or so by the time I left the Air Force Academy. It was an odd, coming-and-going type thing. I was grateful to Perkins for taking me by the scruff of the neck and dragging me back into pro football. Now I was grateful to him for leaving the Giants.

It was on that trip that I told him he'd be back in pro football within five years. In my mind, he was just a pro coach. I wasn't sure he did the right thing at the time, going to Alabama and replacing the Bear. Talk about a tough act to follow. But I think he did a hell of a job there.

What happened to Ray at Alabama, I think, is what happens to a lot of people. He figured he was going home. He figured home was going to be just like it was when he left, the way he remembered it. And it never is.

I was home, though. Just up the hill from the home of the former Ida Naclerio.

Of course I knew being a hometown boy wasn't going to cut me a bit of slack if I couldn't do the job. Getting home was one thing.

The trick was going to be staying there. And I almost didn't.

12

George
and Me

George Young and I are living proof that a general manager and a coach don't have to love each other to work well together.

I think George and I work very well together.

But we're never going to go on outings together, okay?

George had worked for the Dolphins and Baltimore Colts then Dolphins again before coming to the Giants almost as a compromise candidate when Well and Tim Mara couldn't get together on who should run the football operation. In his pro football career, he had worked in both the front office and as a field coach.

While at Baltimore, he had been offensive coordinator when Howard Schnellenberger was head coach.

And I believe it was Schnellenberger that George wanted to coach the Giants, one year after George had hired me. He denied it. Denies it to this day. My information, without betraying any longtime confidences, is that he wanted Schnellenberger pretty bad. It pissed me off at the time, because even though the Giants were finishing off a 3–12–1 season for me, I don't believe one season is a fair shot for any coach in the NFL.

It wouldn't have been a fair shot for me. I don't think Giants history would have been exactly the same without me around after 1983.

In retrospect, I understand it a lot better. I don't like it much. I don't like what George tried to do. The whole thing could have been handled better. But George was trying to save his own job at the time. Schnellenberger was his friend. Schnellenberger had walked in and turned around the University of Miami program. A month after George started courting him, Schnellenberger would win the national championship at Miami, beating Nebraska in the Orange Bowl thanks to a quarterback named Bernie Kosar.

George has always been pretty solid when it comes to working the newspaper guys. He's not a bad politician. But while he was saying "No way" to the Schnellenberger rumors, I was getting different information. I had him meeting with Schnellenberger. A lot.

I figured they weren't drawing up a game plan for Nebraska.

George and I never discussed it. Toward the end of the season, we had a meeting, and I asked him if I was coming back, and he told me we'd talk about it after the season. I don't know what the reason is, but Schnellenberger (he's at the University of Louisville now) turned the Giants down. And I got to stay.

Trust me on all this.

Do I harbor a grudge against George Young? I don't. I was a rookie head coach, I was scared I was going to lose my job, I was mad as hell that this stuff was going on behind my back. And you know what? I got over it. I found out who my friends were. Dan Henning called and offered me that job with the Falcons. Al Davis was on the phone with me all the time, giving me pep talks, telling me not to do or say anything stupid.

Al has this great expression: "If you really want to fight, take it out in the street."

He told me not to take this fight in the street, because if I did, then I was going to lose my job for sure.

The bottom line is that I kept my job. And George and I have worked well together ever since, and we both must be doing something right because here we are, champions of the world. The big new football expression is "We're on the same page." Well, when it comes to personnel matters, George and I are on the same page. He's always been a buffer between me and the owners. He's backed me when I asked to go after high-priced backup players like Ottis Anderson.

We've never had a big disagreement when it came to a draft.

He goes about his business. I go about my business. We're not buddies. Big deal. Al has another thing he's said to me about a million times: "You just coach your goddam team." He's right again. Things are going to happen. You're not going to be madly in love with your general manager.

Coach the team.

You got problems, cry yourself to sleep.

So I put all that stuff with George and Schnellenberger behind me because it wasn't going to help me coach the Giants. To this day, it's never come up in a conversation. I don't care anymore about why and how and why not or any of that.

I'm still here and George is still here, and we're both probably going to be here for a long time.

It's just that he almost didn't give me a second chance after 1983.

I'll level: I think George is happy with the way things turned out.

And I definitely know he got lucky.

13

●

3-12-1

But then again, everybody makes mistakes.

Like I said, my first big move as head coach of the Giants was to bench the quarterback—Phil Simms—who later helped me look like a genius when we won the Super Bowl.

Actually, though, Ray Perkins was set to bench Simms in favor of Brunner in the 1982 preseason. Brunner was the one who'd quarterbacked the Giants into the playoffs. Simms was having one injury after another. Ray had a lot of feeling for Phil, because it had been Ray's decision to make him the No. 1 draft choice when not too many people knew about this quarterback from Morehead State in Kentucky.

Still, after the Giants-Steelers preseason game in 1982, Ray told the staff that he'd made up his mind about the quarterbacks, and he was giving the job to Scott

Brunner. I'm not trying to lay my decision off on Ray's decision. I'm not sure he was locked in. He might have changed his mind about Simms and Brunner before the start of the regular season.

But he didn't have to. Simms' knee made up Perkins' mind, and Brunner was the man.

Now it was a year later and I had the same choice to make. There are a lot of things a new coach doesn't need, and a quarterback controversy is one of them. Stepping into one of those is just stepping into a pile of shit.

Except I've got a problem: I don't know a lot about Phil Simms. I'd seen him have eight really good games in 1981, but after he went down, Brunner did a hell of a job the second half of the season. And even though Brunner didn't set the world on fire in 1982, I didn't have a big problem with him, and I thought he'd looked solid enough in spots. I know that doesn't sound like the greatest endorsement in the world, but with Brunner I knew. With Simms, I didn't know, at least not enough. Brunner, in my mind at the time, was the proven commodity and Phil just wasn't, not after a year-and-a-half off.

I came to training camp with an open mind. Simms could have convinced me with his play that he ought to have the job. If he won a clearcut decision, it was his. That wasn't the way things worked out in the 1983 preseason. I didn't see a lot to choose from between Brunner and Simms.

Neither one of them jumped out and said, "Hey, I'm better than he is."

I was more familiar with Scott Brunner. I felt the team was more familiar with Brunner. I announced that Brunner was the man. And Phil Simms didn't like it one bit. He's always been competitive, he was itchy as hell after being on the sidelines all that time, he felt the job belonged to him before he got hurt and now he was healthy and he wanted the sonofabitch back.

Phil came to my office and said, "Is this the way things are going to be?"

I told him why I'd done it. He just kept shaking his head.

"I want you to trade me then," he said finally.

We talked a little more, but I couldn't move him off the idea of being traded. I didn't think he meant it in his heart.

But you never know.

"If I can't be a starter," he said, "then I'd just as soon be someplace else."

We were getting nowhere, but Phil did seem calmer when he walked out the door than when he'd walked in. We'd never have that trade conversation again. As it turned out, Brunner got off to a mediocre start. So did the team. We lost to the Rams at home. Then we beat Atlanta in Atlanta, lost to Dallas in Dallas, beat up Green Bay at home, lost to San Diego.

The next week we were losing to the Eagles at Giants Stadium. I made the move to Simms.

He completed four out of his first five passes and the team was excited and the crowd was excited. I was a little excited, to tell you the truth. We had been struggling to that point, but if we could beat the Eagles, we would have been 3–3 going into the meat of the schedule.

Simms went down with a compound fracture of his thumb.

Out for the season.

Third season in a row.

I felt bad for him and worse for me. Because the end result was that I had really screwed up my offense. I had hurt Brunner's confidence by benching him early in the season in favor of Simms. Then with Simms out, and Brunner back in, I had hurt the confidence of the team in Brunner. He was only back in there because the other guy got a thumb. We lost to the Eagles. It would be six weeks before we beat anybody.

By then, the Giants' records was 2–8–1. The only thing that stopped the string of losses was a tie with the Cardinals that was one of the ugliest games of all time, one no team seemed capable of winning.

The only game we'd win after Simms' injury was the Eagles game in November.

By then, George Young was hunting around in his black book for Howard Schnellenberger's phone number.

What was supposed to be the best year of my life turned out to be the worst.

The year out of football in Colorado had been a picnic compared to 1983.

I think people had gotten the idea that even with the 4–5 record and not making the playoffs in the strike season that things were headed in the right direction with the Giants, and it didn't take me long to find out they weren't. Maybe I had kidded myself a little bit that I didn't need to make radical changes, because things hadn't fallen completely apart.

But as it turned out, radical changes did need to be made. By the time the next season started—after I had survived George Young's cut—twenty-two players would be gone from the 1983 squad.

You make changes like that, you make them for all kinds of reasons. I thought guys were getting old at a couple of important positions. For instance, 1983 would be the last Giant season for Kelley and Van Pelt at linebacker. And there were guys I just thought would never play for me the way I wanted them to play.

The writers like to make fun of how I'm always talking about "my guys."

Well, I had to get rid of the ones who weren't *ever* going to be my guys.

It didn't take me too long into 1983 to also realize that some guys weren't going to be around next year because they were using drugs. Now I didn't know a hell of a lot about the subject then. It was 1983, and being a head coach, that forced me to begin educating myself about drugs, and users, and how I was going to deal with the whole stinking problem. I'll talk more about that later, as it related to Lawrence, and the other Giants who dealt with their drug problems and stayed around, or didn't deal with the problem, or didn't stop using, and were finally told to get lost.

(You get more than one chance with me. But if you don't learn, or don't want to learn, and you can't stay clean even though you know it's going to cost you your career and maybe your stinking *life*, then you eventually are going to hear this in my office: "Go get your stuff and get out of here."

And they'll say, "But coach...."

"Get your stuff and get out of here.")

I wasn't an expert in '83, and there was a hell of a lot

going on, but I had eyes and ears, and I knew drugs were around. And I was smart enough to know that if I didn't find a way to deal with the problem, it could help get me fired.

You try to help people first of all, but drugs will get a coach's ass fired, no doubt in my mind.

There's a coach I tried to tell, because the word was out about his team, and he just didn't want to hear it.

He got fired.

He called me up when it was too late and said, "I should have listened."

I didn't have an epidemic or anything like that, and it wasn't the reason we were 3–12–1, but drugs were around, and I knew it. So there was that, and some guys getting on in years, and the fact that I thoroughly messed up the deal with Brunner and Simms, and injuries. Carpenter went down with a knee, a lot of guys went down.

We tried to lead the world in turnovers.

We didn't have a running game after Carpenter hurt his knee.

Even Lawrence wasn't showing up to do it every Sunday the way I thought he should, despite the fact that he was all-World and all that again.

I didn't feel there was much team unity, the whole goddam thing just wasn't hanging together the way it should have, which was probably as much my fault as anyone else's.

You'd be amazed at how a 3–12–1 season will just fall right into place when you've got all that shit going on. Al kept telling me, "Just coach your goddam team."

And I was trying like hell. It just didn't work.

There was too much that needed fixing, and sixteen games wasn't enough time.

The last game of the season, against the Redskins at RFK Stadium, *was* the season. The defense played great. We led 19–7 in the third period. Lawrence was all over the place. Then Jeff Rutledge, who I'd put in there at quarterback to finish out the season, fumbled a couple of times and they got some easy points, and we ended up losing 31–22.

It was December 17, 367 days since George Young had called me into his office and offered me the job. Now I was hearing about him and Schnellenberger, and I was wondering if my days were numbered.

In 1983, football wasn't even the worst of it, that's maybe the most amazing part.

Bob Ledbetter, my backfield coach, dropped dead of a stroke in October. He was a friend, a terrific coach. It was obviously a shock to me and everyone in the organization.

His dying was only the beginning.

My father had open-heart surgery later on that same month.

In December, Doug Kotar, who'd been a fine, fine Giants running back in the '70s and one of the most respected players in the history of the organization, finally died after a long fight against brain cancer. Kotar still had many friends on the team, and while his death had been expected for a long time, it threw a pall over the last weeks of an already depressing season. We went as a team to his funeral in western Pennsylvania.

My mother came down with cancer. She'd be dead within a month, and my father would die of complications from his heart problems six weeks later, in February of 1984.

How do you deal with it? You just do. I spent time at the hospital, first with my father, then with my mother, then with my father, and the rest of the time I tried to throw myself into my work, except that the work of finishing out 3–12–1 wasn't exactly like taking your mind off your problems.

From October on, when Bob Ledbetter died, every day was just a battle, one way or another. I'm not trying to glorify it or anything, but it just was. It was a lousy time in my life. Like I said, sometimes things don't look the way you thought they would. I was back in Jersey. I was head coach of the damn *Giants*. And it just seemed like everything had gone completely wrong.

So maybe you understand that I didn't exactly want to run into George Young's office and try to give him a hug when I found out that in addition to all the bad things that were happening in my life, he was scouting Howard Schnellenberger's future plans when he said he was scouting games.

I knew the ownership was disgruntled with the way the season turned out. Obviously, Young was disgruntled with me, because I trusted the information I was getting about him and Howard. Hell, I was disgruntled with the season and with me.

Again: you find out who your friends are.

Like Henning.

I had been named head coach of the Giants about three weeks before he was named head coach of the Falcons (incidentally, if you don't think this is an insane business, consider the fact that Henning would probably have kept his job after last season if the Falcons had won one more lousy game. One. It wouldn't have changed anything about Henning, or the job he'd done. But 8–7–1 would've looked better than 7–8–1. When it became apparent after the Super Bowl that Atlanta liked me a lot, I wanted to say to them, "Hell, this shouldn't even come up because you should've kept Henning"). We just figured it was this fitting thing for our friendship that it had happened for us—head coach in the pros—at the same time in our lives.

So he was right there for me when he found out I was in trouble.

Dan didn't make a big deal about it. The tone of the offer was always, "Yeah, well, if things don't work out with the Giants..."

So I knew I had a job in Atlanta working for him if I wanted it. And there were a few times in late December when I thought about just saying, hell with it, just quit the Giants, and go down and work for Dan.

True.

The funny thing is, the reason I didn't do it *was* Dan. We were talking on the phone one night, going over the same ground about what was happening, and he said, "Hey, what's the worst thing that can happen to you?"

I said, "What do you mean?"

"Just what I said. What's the absolute worst thing that can come out of all this?"

I said, "Well, the worst thing that can come out of this is that I get fired."

Henning said, "Big deal."

And we both laughed.

He was right. I'd been fired before, I'd left places, I'd gone to the *wrong* places, I'd been out of football for a year, and things had still worked out all right. I'd become head coach of the Giants. If I got fired, they couldn't take that away from me. I'd survive. I'd survived in the past. A lot of stuff was ganging up on me, on the field, off the field, the rumors, all of it. It wasn't always going to be that way. I'd keep the job, or I wouldn't. Big deal. Henning helped me a lot with my attitude.

"You just stay in there," he kept saying. "You just be the coach I worked with and the guy I've always known, and things are gonna work out."

It was the same thing Al Davis kept telling me in the dark days. Except that Dan uses nicer language.

14

Al

I first met Al Davis, the smartest man in pro football, at a college all-Star game in Corpus Christi, Texas in 1964. I said I wasn't the greatest player who ever came down the pike, and I was telling the truth, but I had my moments. I did get invited to this all-Star game whose name I can't remember in Corpus Christi, and I did get drafted by the Lions.

And I got to meet Al.

We kid about the game now, because I'm sure he doesn't remember me even if he says he does. I broke my hand on Tuesday—we were playing on Saturday— and it swelled up in this disgusting way, and I finally went to see the doctor. He told me four broken bones, not one, and put a cast on it.

The doctor said, "You still think you're going to play?"

I said, "Might as well play." What the hell, I was twenty-two years old, this was it for my college career, why not play?

Actually, I just wanted to hang around Al a little more. He was from the American Football League and I didn't know too much about that, but he was still the first *pro* coach I'd ever been exposed to. So I was a little more than impressed. Enamored is a better word. Or maybe fascinated. He looked pretty much the same way he does now, with that slicked-back hair, real lean and all that, stalking around. And he was demanding as hell, yelling at guys in that accent of his which is sort of Brooklyn and southern. I thought he was great. It's not like we became instant friends, or anything like that; it wasn't like when I met Mickey. But I watched everything he did on the field, and listened to everything he said, and one night at the hotel, I ended up sitting with him and talking about football for maybe half an hour, and from then on, I was hooked on him. He went his way and I went mine, but I always had a special feeling for the Raiders.

I went a long time without having any real contact with him. I just followed him, and the Raiders, and all the controversy over his fight with Pete Rozelle, the NFL commissioner, about moving the Raiders from Oakland to Los Angeles, and I saw how he kept up this level of excellence with his team no matter what, and how every few years, the Raiders would win the Super Bowl.

I had some friends who worked for the Raiders, guys who I knew from college football. The ones I thought were really good were the ones Al ended up hiring. Never failed. So I felt like I had that contact, and Al and I had some mutual friends, and when things started to go bad in 1983, I just picked up the phone and called him.

And from that time on, he's been a tremendously loyal friend to me. I know all the people in the league who hate Al. I know he's not the most popular person in the history of the world around the Giants. Hell, he's not the most popular person *anywhere*—except with the people who work for him, the people who play for him, the people who root for his team, and his friends. I judge people by who they are, not who other people say they are.

I talk to him all the time. When we talk now, of course, the circumstances are a little more pleasant than they were in 1983. Al's big line for me these days goes something like this: "Am I speaking to the coach of the New *Yawk* Giants, the cradle of professional football?"

There isn't anybody connected with pro football who has the wealth of experience Al Davis does. Not anyone close. He was an assistant coach, he was a head coach, he was commissioner of the American Football League, he's an owner now. He's seen it all. He's done it all. And with all that, Davis has always had time for young coaches. Al likes coaches. It doesn't matter where you come from, it doesn't matter whether you're twenty years younger or the same age as him, he likes guys who like football. And I like football. He determined that right away. I didn't want to be a goddam matinee idol; I just wanted to be a coach.

Al liked that.

My father used to have an expression about how he'd seen a lot of guys leave New York via Madison Avenue. It was something I never forgot. Al knew I didn't want to go Madison Avenue. I just wanted to win.

I've talked to him ever since 1983, in good times and bad. He was there for me in 1984 when things started to get a little better, and he was there when we were closing in on the playoffs in 1985. I talk to him about everything: how to approach a team, how to approach my quarterback when things aren't going well.

I'll say, "What would you do if this happened to you?"

Or: "*Did* this ever happen to you?"

He's always been terrific.

He'll say, "You got problems? Nobody cares. You just figure out a way to win Sunday, or *then* you'll have problems. You just beat those guys." Sometimes he'll look at something from a coach's point of view, and then sometimes he'll fool me and beat me up and look at something from an owner's point of view. His mind is very damn active all the time, and you should never think you have him figured.

A big thing with Al is something he dwells on with me all the time. He says, "Never lose focus of what you're responsibility is. And your basic responsibility is not to make any excuses. Coaching has nothing to do with excuses. You can *always* pick out excuses, a different one every year if you want."

He's right. You can always put your hand on as many excuses as you want. This guy didn't show up. That guy's on dope. My quarterback is hurt. *And nobody cares.*

"You just keep your eye on the eagle," Al likes to say. He means to take what you have every year and find a way to win with it, and keep winning, like the Raiders have done, while he's kept his eye on the eagle all these years.

When it was time to start preparing for the Super Bowl, one of Al's big things was that we should do as much preparation as possible in New *Yawk*—New Jersey, New York, it's all the same to Al.

"It's a fine line," he said. "You got to work like hell before you get out there but don't *over*work, because a lot of Super Bowl coaches have done that and they've lost."

And he said, "You think you're gonna get to do normal work when you get out there, and that's not the way it is."

He was right, of course. Al's been right about a lot of things. I hear a lot of things about him, the way I hear a lot of things about Bob Knight, and they're just not true. Al Davis, to me, is a special guy, and someone who's been an unbelievable natural resource for me, and a lot of other coaches.

To worry about what other people are going to think, to ignore a natural resource like that, you've got to have the world's dumbest ego, or just be a jerk.

And if you're a jerk, then you're never going to be able to keep your eye on the damn eagle.

I love Al Davis.

15

Off the

Ropes

I must have gotten a hell of a lot smarter between the end of the 1983 season and the end of the 1984 season, because by the end of the 1984 season, I had a new four-year contract to be head coach of the Giants.

Once I made the cut, I just decided, "I don't give a damn, I'm gonna do things my way." I'd always been an aggressive person and I'd certainly been an aggressive coach almost from the start, but I thought I'd been strait-jacketed some of that previous season. I wasn't going to make that mistake again. In the end, you've got to be yourself. You can't be Knight. You can't be Al, or Perk, or Tom Landry, or Mickey Corcoran. If you're not comfortable with yourself, don't even bother showing up.

One of the first things I did was hire a strength and conditioning coach named Johnny Parker. It turned out to be one of the best moves I'd ever make as a coach. Parker had been strength coach at South Carolina and Indiana and LSU and finally Mississippi. I interviewed a lot of guys for the job, but he impressed me the most. I'd called Knight about Parker, and Knight said, "It's not work for this guy. He *loves* it."

I just felt I had to do something after all the injuries we'd had in 1983. Over the course of the season, I'd seen twenty-five guys end up on the Injured Reserve list, and I felt like I couldn't sit back, had to attack that baby head on. Parker was my point man. He came in and supervised an off season weight and conditioning program (lifting and running), and he'd eventually supervise the construction of our new weight room at Giants Stadium.

So in the spring of 1984, Parker started that first program, and we had thirty or so guys show up for it and start working out. This was good for two reasons:

1) It helped get the players ready for the season, and into a football mode early;

2) It got them *together.*

As I said, I felt we hadn't hung together very well as a team during all the hard times of the previous season. I felt if we were going to have any chance in the NFC East, we did have to be stronger in all ways, and that included team unity.

Eventually, the new weight room would probably do more to foster the unity than anything. More than anything else, it has become a symbol of the Giants' unity. It is a players-only place (well, players and coaches). People are always wandering in and out of the locker room; not the weight room. It is part clubhouse, part frat house. I think Johnny has given out everything except secret decoder rings. I didn't know it would end up this way, but it did, and I'm glad.

(I might add that the weight room also cost Well Mara and Tim Mara a couple of hundred thousand dollars in the long run, but I presented the proposal to George Young and he presented it to them, and if either of the Maras ever said boo about that, I never heard about it. Like everybody else, I used to hear that stuff about how "The Maras won't spend money to win," but as coach, I just haven't seen any evidence of it. I don't want them to give me an apple. It's just the way things are.)

I'm not saying that everybody on your football team has to love each other. Or pal around with each other. Or have cookouts at a different house every weekend. But it sure doesn't hurt if they *like* each other. You don't want cliques on your team if you can help it, you don't want any damn black-white splits, you don't want bickering. It's just like any other business: As boss, you want to create the best possible environment in the workplace. These past few seasons, we've been tremendously lucky with the Giants, because the personality of the team seems to almost demand friendship among the players. And that goes back to veterans like George and Harry and Phil and Burt and Benson and Hunt and Tony Galbreath. Rookies come in, free agents come in, and they don't have to be damn rocket scientists to observe that people act a certain way around here and things are done a certain way around here, and any boat rocking probably won't be appreciated a whole hell of a lot.

The conditioning program, and the weight room, really helped with all that, though I never could have seen it coming to this degree. I can walk downstairs from my office in the middle of March and find thirty-five to forty members of what you call your world champions just busting their asses, not even two months removed from Super Bowl XXI.

Sometimes you can't plan these things. You just fall out of a tree and land on your feet.

T he team that would beat the Broncos in Pasadena really began to take shape during the 1984 season. I knew when 1983 ended that I would have to make changes, and half the 3–12–1 team ended up being gone. And the guys who made *my* cut began to change the face of the New York Giants.

I found out a lot of things in 1984.

I found out I had one hell of a quarterback in Phil Simms, and I wasn't going to have to worry about that position again, as long as he stayed out of the emergency room.

Halfway through the season, I benched Butch Woolfolk and put little Joe Morris at halfback, and found out I had misjudged Joe the way a lot of people had. He wasn't too small. He was a lot of heart and skill and moves and speed and strength just stuffed inside a five-foot-seven package. It was toward the end of that season I realized Joe was going to be one of the best.

I found out Zeke Mowatt was more than a tight end with some talent, but a guy who liked the game the way I liked the game, and couldn't get enough work, brute work or otherwise. Zeke would become Phil's favorite receiver during that season (and Zeke would come back this season from a bad knee injury suffered the year before. He became our other tight end along with Mark Bavaro; I might have been happiest about Zeke's touchdown catch in the Super Bowl, because I knew how far he had come to catch that ball).

So Phil established. Joe emerged. So did Zeke. So did Carl Banks, who began to first show all that talent. We had a couple of rookie wide receivers to help Lionel Manuel. The defensive backfield began to form, in the persons of Terry Kinard and Perry Williams and Kenny Hill, the Yalie who'd come over from the Raiders the year before. Hill hadn't played a lot for the Raiders, but he had two Super Bowl rings, and I thought he brought as much to the locker room as he did to the field.

Things began to organize. It happens. Leonard Marshall and Jim Burt took their places alongside George in the defensive line. And slowly, as the guys got to know each other, the offensive line began to develop, especially in the persons of Chris Godrey, kid who'd come over from the United States Football League, and Karl Nelson, big second-year man out of Iowa State.

But it took time for the offensive line. While it did, there were times I was worried that Phil Simms might get killed back there, get knocked on his ass and just not get up (it had happened before, in those seasons when he was having that unbelievable string of bad luck and bad timing). He didn't have much of a ground game until Joe Morris came running in from the bench later in the season. He had baby receivers, learning the ropes.

What he mostly had was Zeke.

And Simms was great.

I mean, *great.*

He never bitched about protection. They knocked him down, he got up, he kept throwing the ball all over the joint. He opened the season by throwing for 409 yards against the Eagles, and all he went on to do from there was break the Giants records for pass completions and pass attempts and yardage. I happen to think Simms' attitude was a little like mine for 1984—he didn't give a shit, he was just going to show everybody what they had been missing in those seasons when he'd been hurt.

In the third game of the season, he went for about 350 yards against the Redskins, but we lost.

So he came back later and came within a yard of 400 and we beat the Redskins 37–13.

Later on, we were trailing the Kansas City Chiefs 27–14 late in the game. Simms said, Okay. He went to work. We won 28–27.

He had something to prove to me, and everyone else. I had something to prove to George Young and everybody else.

We did.

The Giants were 9–5 with two games to go, lost the last two games, made the playoffs as wild card anyway. There was a lot of newspaper talk about how we "backed in" to the playoffs after losing the last two. I guess everybody forgot about 3–12–1 pretty fast. Backed in? My ass. We went out to Anaheim to play the Rams in the wild card, beat them 16–13 by controlling the ball all day long and controlling Eric Dickerson (he'd gained over 2000 yards during the regular season, but we held him to 107, and he never really burned us).

So once again, it was the 49ers in the second round of the playoffs, and a game at Candlestick Park. It would end up being the second time in three years that we'd play the 49ers tough, and they'd go on to win the Super Bowl.

That trend would end the next season, when we beat San Francisco 17–3 in a wild card game at Giants Stadium.

But then, we've been ending a lot of bad Giants trends lately, you know?

W e had played the 49ers during the regular season, and they'd beaten us 31–10 at home. On a Monday night. And the score was 21–0 in the first quarter.

I would have switched to another channel if I could have, but I had to stay and watch the whole thing.

I think if we had played the San Francisco 49ers ten times that season, we would have lost eight times.

But I thought one of the two times we could have won came at Candlestick Park. We got behind 14–0 early to Joe Montana and the boys. The only touchdown we scored all day came on an interception by Harry Carson. Still, we got the score back to 14–10.

They scored before the half on a touchdown pass to Freddie Solomon, and it was 21–10.

It ended up 21–10.

We just weren't ready to win that type of game against that type of opponent. We kept trying. We would end up having the ball inside the 49ers' thirty-yard line five times in that game, and we never scored an offensive touchdown. I kept thinking that if we could score just once, get it to 21–17 in the second half, then all the pressure would shift to them, because they were supposed to be the best team in the NFL, they were *supposed* to win the game, and now it looked like they might not be able to do that.

It never happened. Another Giants season ended at Candlestick Park.

I was angry that we lost, mostly because I think the 49ers were ready to be taken in the second half and we just could not get it done. It happens that way sometimes. But the ending felt more like a beginning. When I took the head job after the 1982 season, I felt Giants fans were wrong to think the team was headed in the right direction.

I felt differently after 49ers 21-Giants 10. We had made the playoffs, we had won a playoff game, we had won ten games in all. I had a quarterback. I had an offensive line at the end of the season, something I didn't have at the start of the season. I had Banks, who looked like a trainee who was going to grow up to be LT. I had a young defensive backfield.

I had one other thing going for me, most important thing of all:

Confidence in myself.

I felt I could do the job. I had done things my way in 1984, and we had turned the disaster of 1983 around. I had cleared away some of the deadwood. I was starting to surround myself with my guys. I had asserted myself more. I felt like I was in charge.

And we had won more games than we lost. It was my first winning season as a head coach.

I'd been 4–7 at Air Force.

I'd been 3-12-1 with the Giants.

We still hadn't done anything great yet, but we were winning again.

What the hell, I was on a roll. When I got the new contract, I wanted to start the new season in February.

16

Close,
But No Cigar

Sunday, January 5, 1986.

The second-round playoff game between the Bears and the Giants has been over a few minutes. The scoreboard still says "Chicago 21, New York 0" and the score is going to stay that way forever. The Bears would go on from there to trample the Rams and demolish the Patriots in the Super Bowl, and everybody would start calling them one of the great teams of all time. And maybe they were.

I don't care about any of that in the visiting locker room at Soldier Field.

I'm a little more than disappointed that we lost.

I'm *pissed*.

It was a lot like the situation the season before against the 49ers, and not just because the Bears would end up winning the Super Bowl just like the 49ers had. The

Bears were better. If we had played the Bears ten times, it would have been the same deal I saw with the 49ers in '84: the Bears would more than likely have beaten us eight.

But now the game has been played, and I feel like January 5, 1986, could have been one of the two my guys won.

It's the beauty of sports. The other team can be better, but you can be better *that day*. The Bears had a defense? Well, *I* had a defense too. I felt like the sides were pretty much even there. I figured if we could get on top early, put a touchdown up there, we could win. Again: the beauty of sports. You don't have to be better yesterday, or tomorrow. Just today. Just beat those guys today.

We got shut out. The only score of the first half came when a fierce Chicago wind blew the ball away from Sean Landeta, and he just whiffed it, and Shaun Gayle of the Bears picked it up and ran five yards for a touchdown. We looked to be driving pretty well the first time we had the ball, and then Rob Carpenter fumbled. When the Bears scored a couple of touchdowns in the third quarter we were dead, because you just can't come from behind against them, not that Sunday, not against that defense.

21–0.

And I'm upset.

The game had ended, and I hadn't said a word to anybody on the sidelines. I got into the locker room and I still wasn't talking. Some guys came up, you know, from the organization, and they're saying, "Good year, good year, get 'em next year," and I'm just saying, "Yeah, yeah" and really wanting to blow them off. I don't want to talk to the players, I don't want to talk to my coaches. I just felt we had blown a great chance. And I was well aware that there was no guarantee that we would ever get this close again. You *never* know. As soon as the gun went off, I started thinking about that, asking myself the questions that coaches must ask themselves in all sports when they don't win the big goddam game:

Was this the best shot I'm going to have?

Was this the team I was supposed to do it with?

Could this have been our season instead of theirs?

There was no cooling-off period; the questions started to eat me up right away. I left the locker room, I did my press conference, I came back to the locker room. And I still wasn't talking to anybody.

Except George Martin and Harry Carson.

They had been through more Giants wars than anybody else. They had come the furthest to this game. This had been their best shot, at least so far, and they weren't getting any younger, and they didn't know if there would be another chance, or if this was their last chance.

I told them both the same thing:

"We just blew a big chance, but we're gonna get another one, I *promise* you. We're gonna figure out a way to get this thing done next year. I can't guarantee you that we're gonna get there. But we're *gonna* get there. We're gonna figure out a way to win this game instead of lose it. I'm sick and stinking tired of one win and go home in the stinking playoffs."

Or words to that effect.

I felt bad for myself; I felt worse for them. They had been out there for a long time, through all those losing Sundays at the end of the '70s, laying it on the line for the New York Giants. They had provided a sort of leadership for me that coaches only dream about in their locker rooms. I wanted all our players and coaches to win. But I felt a special bond with Harry and George. That's why I felt like I had to promise them at least one more chance.

More guys came up and said, "Good season."

I kept saying, "Yeah, great, thanks a lot."

I was still thinking about Carpenter's fumble and Landeta's whiff in the wind, and the way things just got away from us in the third quarter, and us not being able to stop their rush once they teed off on Simms. They were better, and they were playing at home in weather they liked, but we could have been better *today*, and we weren't.

"Great season, coach. Lemme shake your hand."

"Yeah, right, thanks."

Mickey was with me, as usual, because he's around the team a lot and still the same guidance counselor for me that he's always been. Mickey could see I didn't want to talk. So he didn't talk. He just took it all in. He knew what I was thinking. He knew the opportunity we'd had.

The guys showered, and got dressed. The writers finally left the locker room. The equipment and the uniforms got packed, and it all looked like it does after any road game, except that the season was over, and we weren't going to get a crack at the Bears or anybody for eight months. Looking ahead to September, it seemed like eight years.

I didn't talk on the bus ride to O'Hare Airport and I didn't talk to anybody as we boarded, and by then everybody except Mickey was steering pretty clear of me. All in all, it was probably three hours by now since the game had ended.

The plane took off. I had a beer, and then I had another, and I could feel a little of the tension drain out of me.

But not too much.

Still, it was enough that Mickey Corcoran, who knew how to win and how to lose, felt that conversation might be a possibility now, instead of cause for a potential homicide.

When he did talk, it was pure Mickey. He didn't waste a lot of time with preliminaries, because he never has.

Mickey just wanted to talk about what he always did: Winning.

He said, "You got to figure out a way to beat those goddam guys."

The plane was over Pittsburgh at the time. The pilot said something about that over the speakers.

I looked at Mickey and smiled.

"Hey, Mick. They're pretty good, you know."

Mickey said, "I know that. But you had a chance to do something today, and you didn't do it, so it's up to you to figure out a way to do better with your next chance, if you get one. And you'll probably have to beat these guys, so you better start thinking of a way to do it."

It was pretty much the same message I had given to George, and to Harry. I had learned my lessons well from Mickey.

"I told George and Harry they'd get another chance," I said.

Mickey said, "Now you just go make sure you're right about that."

The plane wasn't even to Newark, and Mickey and I

had already put our feet down firmly in next season. See, he knew why I so upset.

Mickey knew I'd had it in my head all year long that maybe the Giants could win the Super Bowl.

It had been an unusual season, 1985, filled with good and bad, the way most of them are. In training camp, I had to make perhaps the toughest cut I've ever made with the Giants, when I chose Landeta over Dave Jennings.

Jennings had been the punter for ten years. He had been a tremendous performer over those years, kicking himself into the record books, to the point where even if he'd retired after leaving the Giants (instead of going on to a second career with the Jets), I think Dave Jennings would have been remembered right then as one of the great punters of all times, and an artist at painting the ball somewhere inside the ten-yard line. It's a mouthful, but it's true. He'd always been a terrific spokesman for the Giants, he was popular with the fans. He was the kind of person you want in the locker room.

But Landeta, another guy we got from the USFL, was younger, with a stronger leg. What was in back of Dave Jennings was in front of him.

Still, it was the hardest cut of all. I'll do all the work that coaching involves. I'll put in the hours, and I'll work like a madman helping us get ready for the draft, and I'll travel, and draw up game plans, and figure out ways to overcome injuries.

I won't complain.

You come in and make the cuts for me, especially when they touch someone like Dave Jennings.

When Jennings did hook on with the Jets after leaving us, I'm sure he was the happiest man in football, his career being extended that way.

I was the second happiest. I wished he would have shared Super Bowl XXI with us.

We did a lot of things right in 1985. Phil continued to be, in my mind, one of the top quarterbacks in the game. Joe Morris became on of the top running backs in the game.

Morris ran for over 1300 yards.

He scored twenty-one touchdowns.

He had a two-hundred-yard day against the Steelers.

He ran for over one-hundred yards seven different times.

He gave Simms the kind of running game he'd never had with the Giants.

If there were still people out there who thought that Joe Morris was still small at five-foot-seven, he showed them. And kept showing them. We all found out why he had broken all those rushing records at Syracuse University that had belonged to people like Jim Brown and the late Ernie Davis, Jim Nance and Larry Csonka. He just brought a new look, a whole new dimension, to our offense. Phil was the same player he'd always been, but given some help with the run, he ended up in the Pro Bowl.

We were very close to being an outstanding team.

We weren't because we didn't play well enough under pressure from the beginning of the season to the end. The word choke is too strong. Hell, we ended up 10–6 in the regular season, and then we messed up the 49ers 17–6 in the wild card game.

But we didn't win the NFC East, which we should have. The six games we lost, we lost by a total of twenty points. *Twenty.* Average it out if you want. Do the arithmetic. The most points we lost any game by was seven, against the Cowboys in the second-to-last game of the regular season, with the division title on the line.

We lost to the Packers by three.

The Cowboys by one.

The Bengals by five.

The Redskins by two.

On and on. We were close to being the Bears that season, but we weren't. Whatever those final qualities are that champions are supposed to have, we didn't have. It wasn't just the offense, or the defense. If we needed to fumble a snap and lose, we'd do that. If the other team needed to drive down the field in the last minutes and beat us, they would.

But even with all that, I thought we could get our collective acts together for the playoffs, and when we took care of the 49ers in the first playoff game, I thought we might be on our way to fooling people and beating the Bears.

Bears 21, Giants 0.

Then came the big chill by me towards everybody at Soldier Field.

Then came the plane ride home, when Mickey and I got to work on next season. As it turned out, we wouldn't have to beat "those guys" next season.

But only because we didn't play them.

The close losses, the playoff win over the 49ers (finally) and the loss to the Bears weren't all that happened in 1985.

Because it was during the 1985 season, watching things happening on the field and off it, that I realized there was a problem with Lawrence Taylor. I thought it might be drugs, even if I didn't want to think it might be drugs.

All the signs were there.

He wasn't the same No. 56 on the field.

You're probably thinking, "Should a good-looking player like this have been a tight end for the Giants, or an outside linebacker?" He just looks like future coaching material to me.

I've just returned to Wichita State to coach. I don't know why my jacket says "Hocker." And please notice the pants, because people say I dress funny on the sidelines *now*.

This is supposed to be a photograph of a dashing new assistant coach at the United States Military Academy. Instead, I think I look more like a minor league umpire.

More pictures from Army. It wasn't a staff you'd have wanted to go up against in a streetfight. The Don Shula-look-alike kneeling next to me is Bob Mischak, who's with the Raiders now.

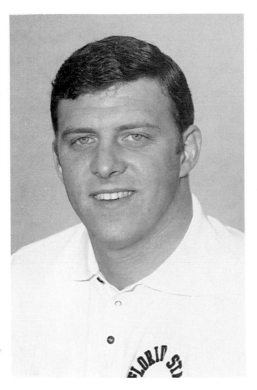

It was at Florida State that I got my first real taste of recruiting. I hated it. To this day, you give me a city in the U.S., I'll tell you the high schools where the players are. *(Courtesy Florida State University)*

The staff at Texas Tech. That's head coach Steve Sloan, a guy I followed around for a while, standing. Fifth from the right is Romeo Crennel, my Giants special teams coach.

We were 4-7 my one season at Air Force. I was afraid I was staring at a lot of 4-7 seasons. When I looked down the road, I thought attendance was always going to be the way it was in this picture. *(Courtesy Sports Information Office, U.S. Air Force Academy)*

We've won the Super Bowl, so I can smile for the first time all week. And not worry about the weather. My wife's smile, as usual, lights up the room, and the party.

The new head coach of the Air Force
Academy. Standing near my left shoulder
is my first recruit. I would have liked him
better if he were a defensive end.
*(Courtesy Sports Information Office, U.S. Air
Force Academy)*

The three darlings—Dallas, Suzy and Jill—at Suzy's wedding in May of 1986. My players make me look good as a coach. My daughters make me look good as a father.

I'm not sure if I'm telling them this is "Sew up your skirts time, girls." But I am a little testy about something. You can tell from the look on Harry Carson's face (No. 53), it is not a Gatorade moment. *(Photo by Fred Roe)*

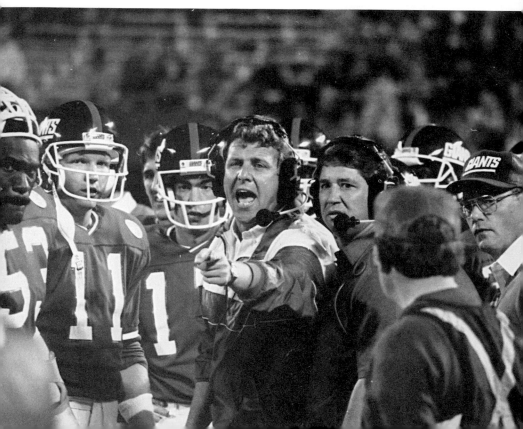

I don't go in much for awards. I don't go in much for seeing my mug on the message board at Giants Stadium. Those people paid good money for playoff tickets, and they have to look up at *me*? *(Photo by Fred Roe)*

My first move as Giants head coach was to bench Phil Simms. We both got over it. And when it came time to play a Super Bowl, Phil silenced all his critics by damn near throwing a perfect game. *(Photo by Fred Roe)*

The moment that became the signature of the Super Bowl champions. That's Harry with the bucket, me trying to assume the tuck position, and Carl Banks (58) apparently trying to get an assist. *(Photo by Fred Roe)*

17

The Fans Don't Care If You Lost Because of Drugs

Might as well make it like one of those delightful press conferences I have all the time:

Question: Where did Lawrence Taylor go for drug rehabilitation?

Answer: None of your goddam business.

Q: How come you don't like talking about Lawrence's drug problem?

A: Because it's not fair to single him out. I've got other guys on my team right now who've been through the same thing. I'm still pissed that it got out on Lawrence, because with the Giants we try to keep things to the Giants.

Q: You got other guys on the Giants who've been through rehab?

A: Some.

Q: Who are they?

A: None of your goddam business.

Q: Coach, don't you think the public has a right to know?

A: No. I love the fans. I love Giants fans. The fans make the game. The fans pay for everything, and I'm grateful to them. But this is not public property, my football team. This is private enterprise. The fans are entitled to the best product I can put on the field every Sunday, week in and week out, year in and year out if I'm lucky. How I put that product out there is my damn business. Is substance abuse a problem for me? You bet your ass it is, and it can get me fired if I don't get off *my* ass and learn something about it and do something about it.

And understand: First things first. I don't want to make myself out to be a humanitarian, because I'm not. But these players are people, and without sounding sappy I care about them as people, and if I've got even a small chance to get them off that shit, I've got to try. I've helped save some people. And I've failed with people. Like I said, don't ever tell me that the Maras are cheap, because I've spent thousands and thousands of dollars trying to help some people, and they've never said a word about the cost.

So they're people first. But they're players too. If I don't keep them playing their best, or replace them with guys who will (and are clean), then I'm an idiot, because I'm taking food out of the mouth of my family, and the mouths of my coaches' families. And I've got a responsibility to them as people too.

Did Lawrence have a problem? Yeah, he had a problem. Only Lawrence and the doctors know the extent of it (here again, I think the public perception was much worse than the reality of it). Did I see it coming on over a few seasons? Yeah. I saw *something*. I was probably slower to pick up on it with Lawrence. I've gotten a lot faster with players. I know the signs. I know what the hell I'm supposed to be looking for. But Lawrence was such a great player, he could slip and *still* be a great player. I probably cut him more slack than I have with other guys. That's my fault. Maybe if I'd been quicker, and confronted him...shit, who knows?

He had set a high standard for so long. But then you start to see inconsistencies. You see other teams dealing with him a little differently, and him handling it a little less *intensely* than he had when he first came into the league. They were inhibiting him with things he would have laughed at earlier in his career. So over a period of time, yeah, I started having concerns about him.

But as I said: Him and others.

It's not just Lawrence; it's gotten to the point where you've got to be suspicious of everyone. Or aware. Or vigilant. Still, you've got to be careful how you handle it.

You better have a game plan for dope, is what I'm saying.

You can be suspicious as hell, but it doesn't mean you can go around pointing your finger all the time because then you're going to turn your locker room into a battlefield. It's going to be you against them, and you'll end up losing your job and not helping anybody.

I will say this about Lawrence: When the time came to do something, he did it on his own, and he did it quietly. I didn't do it. His family didn't do it. His agents didn't do it. Lawrence went off and did it.

Now we all were giving him the same message at that point in time. The message was: "This shit can't go on much longer." He was getting that from all sides. But the decision, the steps toward treatment—he took them himself. He did it without the media finding out too, which helped immeasurably in the long run.

I got sick to my stomach when I watched the media circus and the public circus of Gooden showing up at that Smithers treatment place in New York City when his problem came out. I was sitting watching the news and I yelled to Judy, "Come here and watch this."

She came in from the other room. The pictures on the television said everything. Cameras. Reporters. Cheering fans. Gooden getting out of some van and looking like he just wanted to die.

Judy said, "This is obscene."

I said, "You got that right."

So Lawrence came back. He and I have been very close throughout his career, but toward the end of the 1985 season, he was staying away from me, almost like he was hiding, maybe because he thought I knew him so well. We've never talked about it in those terms, but others have told me he didn't want to hurt me.

When he came back, I told him to just play football and I'd do my best to take care of everything else. My job—as a coach and as a friend—is to create the best possible environment for him at that point.

So here we were at training camp at Pleasantville. We'd been there about two weeks. I was having my little press conference every day. Every day the press conference starts the same way (Lawrence isn't talking. We decided that was best. It's part of my "none of your goddam business" theory about rehab):

"How's Lawrence doing?"

"Lawrence is doing fine."

"What do you mean?"

"I mean Lawrence is doing fine."

After two weeks, I got tired of telling everybody every day that Lawrence was doing fine.

So I finally said, "Hey, there's something else going on here besides Lawrence doing fine, okay? You want to talk about that, we'll talk about that. But I'm not coming in here every day and answering the same stupid questions."

I also think I might have threatened in there to roust everybody with a notebook if they kept bothering Lawrence. The First Amendment wasn't keeping me up nights at that point; I'm trying to win the Super Bowl.

Lawrence, by the way, did just fine all the way through, if you were wondering.

I can't cure the drug problem in society. But I can do my damndest to keep drugs out my locker room and off my team. It doesn't mean I'll succeed, but it's an ongoing struggle.

And the only thing that can ever really work against drugs is mandatory testing.

The Players Association doesn't want to hear about that. No union wants to hear that. Well, I'm sorry, but the hell with them. At least from a coaching standpoint. I know one thing for sure: The Players Association isn't going to care jack if Bill Parcells and his staff get fired over this thing.

The Players Association doesn't care jack about Bill Parcells or his staff, *period*.

Testing is the only way, to save lives and careers. The league and the players can come up with this drug plan and talk about "reasonable cause" all they want, and until teams have the right on their own—without going through the league or the union or anybody—to test and test randomly, the problem is always going to be around, and it's going to stay as deadly and dangerous as it is. There's going to keep being these two-week periods when Gooden goes off to the joint and another baseball player, and a whole damn basketball team like the Phoenix Suns.

I laugh when I hear about invasion of privacy. I mean, I really laugh. I watch John Thompson, the Georgetown basketball coach, and Dean Smith of North Carolina get on television during the Final Four of college basketball, and I hear them talking about how the NCAA drug testing is an invasion of privacy and how upset they are about that, and I just *laugh*. Invasion of privacy? People are *dying* out there. If you break into a burning room and a woman's dress is on fire and you got to rip the dress off to save her, you going to do it? You going to rip it off to save her life?

Shit, you know you're invading her privacy, don't you?

Invasion of privacy.

We're talking about people's lives here.

It's like saying that education is going to be some nuclear weapon against drugs. Hell, these guys have been told all their lives that alcohol and drugs aren't good for them. Trust me on this: I don't ever remember one of my players coming up to me and saying, "Coach, I think drugs are very good for me." And I don't remember one of them ever coming up and saying, "Coach, I think I'm going to drink as much liquor as I possibly can, I can really see it helping my performance this Sunday against the Bears."

Education is important, sure. I've had to educate myself. But it's a baby step. To think that's all you need is ludicrous. It's naive. It's a bunch of shit is what it is. People's lives are what matter. Like I said, I'm not running a mission. I'm not trying to be Sister Bill. But this *is* private enterprise. This is my team. New York Giants. I'm supposed to put a good, productive football team on the field, and win championships if I can, and if drugs can keep me from doing it, then I've got to find a way to correct the problem, or if it persists, eliminate it.

That's why I need testing. And why I've got to be able to have the right to hold up the test results after I've given a guy more than one chance and just say, "Go get your shit and get out of here."

Athletes are not stopping on their own, guys. Neither are hotshots on Wall Street or anyplace else. If you're clean, I'm sorry, I don't see testing as being some sort of terrible hardship. I know tests aren't infallible. I know there are always going to be some problems there.

But do they stack up against Len Bias?

It's an ongoing thing. It's an ongoing thing with the Giants, and every other team that's really paying attention, not sticking heads in the sand over this thing. There are guys we've saved with the Giants, and guys we haven't. The organization, through me, spent nearly $60,000 trying to help one guy, and we failed. Someday I'm going to pick up the paper and find out that he's dead.

We spent $25,000 trying to save another guy.

Failed.

But we've spent rehab money for other guys on the

team, and it's gotten them straightened out and into recovery, and I feel very good about that. I can't stress
enough that I don't think there's anything heroic about
any of it. It's necessary. It's *right*. It's right for the player
who's using, and it's right for the owners and the other
players and the front office and my coaches. If I sit back
and don't do anything, then it's criminal, at least as far as
I'm concerned.

I'd say that in my years as head coach of the Giants,
there's been between twenty and thirty guys who ended
up being asked to leave eventually because of drugs.
Rookies. Free agents. Veterans. Guys whose names would
surprise you and guys whose names wouldn't surprise
you a bit. If they were willing to take help, we did everything we could to get them help.

If not? Go pack your bags, pal, we don't want you
around here.

And all the ones who left had a terrific education
about the perils of drugs. I agree there should be education in the schools. I have never disputed that. But please
don't come in and tell me the answer is having a goddam
seminar for Harry Carson and George Martin. They've
got kids of their own. You're going to tell a thirty-six-
year-old man with teenaged sons and daughter something
he doesn't already know about drugs? *Come on.* These
guys have been through it as parents, the way I've been
through it as a parent. They know. But there's still enough
of them out there who don't care, and don't get scared.

Bias doesn't scare them.

Don Rogers of the Browns dying?

Doesn't scare them.

Even the smart ones are just dumb enough to think

they really are Superman.

The problem is the problem. There are varying degrees to it. Every case is different. There is no way you can be consistent. Al Davis was one of the first owners in professional sports to aggressively attack the problem, to be vigilant about drugs on his team, to talk to experts, to *learn*. I'm trying to do the same thing with the Giants. It's just something else I've picked up from Big Al.

Al says, "Nobody passed any rules that say you have to be consistent."

And Al says, "Your job isn't to be consistent. It's to be *right*." Not just with drugs. With every part of the operation. I've got to do the right thing at the right time for the people I'm responsible to, and the players responsible to me.

After telling you all that, I'll tell you this: The numbers aren't as bad as you think. I know people think that three-quarters of the NFL is taking cocaine or smoking grass, and it's not that way. It's not that way with steroids, either (and don't think I'm not looking for evidence of that the way I'm looking for evidence of sniffers). But volume doesn't define the problem. Repeat: the problem is the problem, whether it's one player, or three, or ten.

I'm very lucky with the Giants, because I've got such great veteran leadership on the team, guys who are role models in the locker room. I've got George. I've got Harry. The young guys come in, they find out right away what George and Harry—and me—think about dope. Right away, a tone is set. The Giants, I think, have a reputation, even for kids coming out of college.

But for me to think it will last forever is naive.

Here's what I should be able to do. I should be able

to call a guy into my office, and the conversation should be able to go like this:

Me: "You using cocaine?"

Player: "Hell, no, coach."

Me: "You're lying. Here's your test results. Your ass is on the street right now."

Player: "Well, coach, I tried the stuff at parties, you know, a couple of times..."

With the truth out, at least we'd have a start, both me and the player. Admission of the problem doesn't mean acceptance. Still: a start. Then I'd get the player right to a doctor. Then we'd both listen to the doctor.

The doctor might say, "He's just messing around, I think he'll stop now. It's not a serious problem right now, but it could be down the road."

Or the doctor might say, "I think he's scared now, and that's a start, but after the season, I think you're going to need treatment to sustain it."

And I'd do my best to help him get the right treatment, whether it's in-patient or out-patient, whatever it takes, quiet as a mouse.

But here's something else I ought to be able to do: I should be able to test that guy at my own discretion once or twice a week. I should be able to walk down to the locker room and say, "Pee in the bottle" through the next season and the season after that if I think it's necessary. It'll be for the guy's own good, whether he wants to believe it or not. I'll be trying to help him save his life. And his career. I'm sorry, but I've got to be able to bust their balls once the problem surfaces. You think football is a bottom-line business? Well, drugs are a lot more of a bottom-line business, and if you don't think that's true, you remember Bias and Rogers.

I think you've got to be able to threaten, to intimidate. The rules are too soft. If I've got a player and a person not going in the right direction, if I see him doing something that's bad for himself or his career—it can be drugs, it can be anything—I've got to be able to step in and take what I think are the proper measures. And mandatory drug testing is the best one I can think of. The damn league is never going to have the people or the facilities or the time or the ability to do the kind of constant testing I think every team needs.

So somebody draw up some intelligent rules so I can take care of it myself.

Please.

And if the players think that's an infringement of their personal rights, then I'll be happy to release them and let them go elsewhere where maybe the coach won't want to interfere with their personal rights.

Then they can help get that coach fired.

I don't want to have the league coming in to bother my players, I don't want strange doctors. I should be able to handle it my own way.

Because all those union guys who scream about infringement of personal rights and the rest of that shit aren't going to run any benefits for the Parcells family when all those players whose right I'm not supposed to infringe on finally wreck my team.

I've made mistakes.

There's a player still on the Giants who I accused of taking drugs, and he wasn't. It took the two of us a while to get over that. Both of us. But even he knew that I was doing it for his own good.

Another guy, I went as far as I could with him. Then I went a couple of more miles. He was talented as hell, and ignorant as hell about drugs. Finally, I had to get rid of him. And I was sad that I failed, because every life is valuable, but I still felt I had to use him as an example.

One of my guys said, "Well, you know he's going to hook on with somebody else."

I said, "You think so?"

I waited a long time, and then the two of us finished that little conversation.

I said, "It's been two years now. You think Joe Blow just isn't answering his phone and missing all those great offers you thought he was going to get?"

What I'm talking about is good business on my part. I'm not kidding about that private enterprise stuff. The Giants aren't Con Edison; if your lights are working, you can't call the Giants to come fix it. I'm trying to do the best I can in my *context*. And I do care about these kids, the ones I've cut and the ones still around. I've seen them cry about our losses and I've seen them bleed for me and I've seen them so cramped up on team flights they couldn't get up out of their seats to go into the bathroom. There's something there between us, beyond business. This is a hard game. Football is a hard life for them, despite all the benefits. I watch these SOB's bust their asses for me week in and week out, and when trouble comes up, whether it's dope or family problems or booze or financial problems, I've got to do what I can. It's a two-way street. They busted their ass for me, I've got to bust my ass for them.

There are no easy answers. Mandatory testing isn't an easy answer, it's just the best one.

The players who are clean, who want to win, they don't want somebody dirty being the reason the Giants don't go all the way. So they'll come knock on my door and say, "Bill, you *got* to do something about this guy, 'cuz he's using."

I tell them I'll get right on it.

My assistant coaches, they've got eyes too. So they'll knock on my door and say, "Bill, I'm worried about sending my kid to college next year, and you want me to coach *this* jerk?"

I've had plenty of those meetings. Hell, the problem is everywhere. I've had guys in the newspaper business come into my office half-bombed on one thing or another. I tell them the same thing I tell my players.

"You're screwing up your life and you know better, so that makes you a jerk."

I can only do what Chubby Parcells used to do with me, whether it was about paying for the car or getting back into college or listening to Mickey Corcoran.

I tell them what the deal is.

If they don't like it, there's the door.

I've learned the hard way. I've talked to drug counselors, I've talked to doctors, I've asked a thousand questions, I've had the doctors challenge me. I couldn't deal with this blindly. And you know what one doctor I respect a lot said to me? "Bust their balls. Ultimately, it's the only thing they're going to understand."

The ones who use cocaine and keep using it don't

understand it's not just their bodies it's working on, it's their *minds*. The drug comes up to them, smiling, and then it owns them. I don't care why a guy used it the first time. Somebody gave it to him at a party. Somebody tried to buddy up to him at a bar or disco, show he could do something nice for a big celebrity football player.

Maybe he thought—correctly—that he might get himself laid if he dropped a little coke on some girl.

That's the beginning. The finish is what I have to deal with: A player spending so much money on coke that he's got money problems and he's bringing them to the field with him. Or a player is falling asleep at meetings, after what was obviously a night—and morning—of hard partying.

I have to deal with that. Or with a subtle drop-off in some guys' performance over a period of time. Or a dramatic drop-off.

And I have to deal with it the right way, under soft rules. I've had to learn about that from doctors and counselors. How rough do you get when you confront an employee? If you make threats, can you back them up? Do I need to call in other people for an intervention? How can I get a guy's attention and keep it?

Do I call his mamma?

You bet your ass I do.

I've done that. More times, I've threatened to do it when somebody wasn't getting the message. And you'd be amazed how well that can work with a certain player, after I've found out one way or another he was using. I swear, sometimes they're more scared about mamma finding out they were sniffing than they are about losing their jobs.

No shit. Sometimes I feel like Dr. Joyce Brothers.

Q uestion: So you think there's ever going to be mandatory drug testing in sports.

Answer: Maybe. Maybe if you've got enough scan-
dals like the one that hit the Phoenix Suns. Maybe if
you've got more Goodens and Taylors. I'm hoping to
God it doesn't take more Len Biases and Don Rogers.
Maybe then the unions will get the idea that we really are
talking about people's lives. After the Suns thing, I heard
the NBA commissioner or somebody say, "Testing isn't
the problem, *drugs* are the problem."

And I laughed like I laughed when I heard John
Thompson and Dean Smith talking about invasion of privacy. Testing is the only chance we've got to get a foothold against drugs, at least in our sector. You've got to be
able to hold those test results up to a player and threaten
him with the loss of his livelihood.

And you've got to be able to use the example of the
guys who are dirty for the guys who are clean, who might
be thinking about giving dope a try.

Because they know it's bad.

Lawrence knew.

The other Giants knew.

Dwight Gooden knew.

Hey, the dead guys knew.

And they went ahead and did it anyway. They say
you can't test guys in the offseason. They say that Bias
and Rogers died in the offseason. I say, Why not? We run
a thirteen week conditioning program with the Giants; it
goes from March nearly to the start of training camp. So

right away, you cut down on the offseason. If you had the rules on your side, and the damn collective bargaining agreement between the players and the owners, you could create a climate where testing felt like it was year-round. Maybe even if a guy was inclined to fool around with the junk, he'd figure it wasn't worth it for a couple of weeks.

Because when he got back to the locker room, here comes Parcells with his trusty Mason jars.

That's what it's going to take. Halfway measures just don't make it. I can't believe the union can't see that. I'm sorry, I really can't believe those guys running the Players Association can oppose mandatory testing in pro football with a clear conscience.

We're talking about people's lives.

No way you can ever say that enough.

18

Every Week Is Boot Camp

Being a narc isn't the job, though.

The job is getting your team ready to win. The hours stink. They just come in and carve up the time you can spend with your family. If you're lucky enough to win the Super Bowl or just play in it, you're in a seven-month season from training camp and then games. Of course, there's the conditioning program for the players before that. You've got the NFL draft in there at the end of April.

Oh yeah. As soon as the Super Bowl ends, they usually bring the top college prospects to a stadium site in that year's designated city, and you go look at the top college prospects.

Vacation? You mean, like a couple of rounds of golf?

All in all, I figure it's great work if you can get it.

Once you're into the season, it seems like next week is starting before last week ends. And last week is a part of next week, because the game you've just played has to be evaluated before you really start preparing for next Sunday's opponent. Or next Sunday *night's* opponent. Or Monday night's opponent. There was a time when the Giants used to play just about all their games at one o'clock on Sunday afternoons. Now that we've won the whole thing, we've become the darlings of the networks. They want to *showcase* us in 1987. So we play three games at one o'clock. The rest of our games are in the doubleheader slot at four on Sundays, or on those new Sunday night games on Sunday night ESPN just got in the new contract, or on Monday night.

Shit, we're practically a new primetime series.

Playing later games won't change the coaches' hours, however. No matter what time we've played on Sunday, or what time we've gotten back from a road game, I'm in my office at Giants Stadium at 6:15 Monday morning. By then, I've made a couple of stops at diners at which I'm a regular. I'd tell you the names of them—they're all in Jersey—except that I'd rather not have a camera crew show up, or turn having coffee with my early-morning pals into some kind of media event.

When I let myself into the Giants' offices and walk down to my own, the tapes from the previous day's game are stacked up and waiting for me. I don't usually watch them in any particular order. They're divided into offense, defense, special teams, and end zone. They've been shot by a wide angle for everything except the end zone plays, which are done in close-up. Whichever part of the game we've had the most trouble with the day before, that's what I'll probably look at first.

It is a time of the day I really enjoy, a part of the week, actually. Football is what I do. Football games are really my office, have been as a coach for going on twenty-five years now. I like looking at the football games. Even if I know there are things in those tapes that are going to make me mad as hell, I enjoy the quiet time with my coffee, my tapes, my remote-control switcher, in the big easy chair in my office.

I don't have a lot of hobbies. So private time like this, even looking at the same game I'd watched from the sideline the day before, is sort of precious to me.

But I do like to look at the bad parts first. If we'd had trouble moving the damn ball in the first half, I'll find that. If we had a breakdown on punt returns, I'll look at that. Or if we gave up a big play on defense, I want to look at it again. And invariably, I'll notice something important I didn't notice the day before.

What I notice will be something about an individual's performance. Good coaches know what the hell is going on during the game. They can *see,* or at least they better be able to see. They know why their teams are having problems during the course of games. Sometimes it takes a while to figure it out from the sideline, but if a coach has to wait and look at the tapes on Monday morning to know what went wrong, that coach is going to lose a whole *pile* of football games.

So if you see in the papers that a coach said, "I'll have to wait and look at the film," you can usually read that a couple of ways:

1) "I don't have a clue what happened on that drive,

but I'm too embarrassed to tell the press."

Or:

2) "I don't feel like answering your question now, so I'm just going to offer the standard coach's answer."

But those tapes can be valuable when it comes to focusing in on one guy. On the sideline, you're usually watching the team. You're looking to see if you have a problem with the offensive *scheme* or the defensive scheme; and if you're having trouble picking it out, you better have first-rate assistants and a proper division of labor so one of them can pick it out for you, depending where the disaster area is. Every guy on the sideline, every coach in the press box, has specific assignments.

I'm not kidding, you better have assistants who are like a team of paramedics. If the Giants start to bleed, we all have got to stop it fast.

Or we'll lose.

When I'm in the office on Monday morning, incidentally, so are my assistants. The offensive guys are looking at the offense, the defensive guys at defense, and so forth. They'll run through their tapes more than once, sometimes three or four times, taking notes the whole time. About eleven, we'll have a staff meeting, talk about why we won or why we lost, who got hurt, things that went wrong, things that have to be corrected before the next game. I'll have seen things they missed, they'll have seen things I missed.

Before noon on Monday, I want the film *dissected,* is what I'm saying.

The injured players have to report by eleven o'clock

on Monday; the doctors look at them, and the ones who need treatment get treatment. Then the whole squad shows up, and every Monday (or Tuesday, if it was a Monday night game), I talk to them about yesterday's game. You better be able to organize your thoughts if you want to coach, and you better be able to communicate. I'll talk for twenty minutes or so about the game, where we are in the season, a lot of the things that my coaches and I have noticed since our dawn patrol began with the tapes.

It's just like Hastings College in there: I don't tell them everything I know. But I tell them enough to get their goddam attention.

Then at one o'clock Monday afternoon, the Giants go to the movies. Everybody gets to look at yesterday's game. Popcorn optional.

They look at the special teams film as a group, then the offense and defense go their separate ways. Between three-thirty and four, we're done with that, and we go out on the field. It's never going to be a very long workout on a Monday, and a lot of times, I'll let the coaches go and just take the team myself, just make the players pay attention to some things I think they should be thinking about during the week.

There's no heavy lifting on Monday. They do some running; Tuesday is a day off. The next time they report is 9:30 Wednesday morning, when the week really begins for the players.

The week never ends for the coaches. For a coach in the National Football League, your week really starts in July and ends in January.

If you're lucky, that is.

Monday is like every other day of the week, in the sense that I meet the gentlemen of the press around noon.

It's probably not in the Top Ten list of favorite parts of my job. But I do it. Now I don't feel that there's any law that says I have to tell the press everything I know. I also don't believe I should lie to them. So somewhere between everything and nothing at all, I try to find a middle ground.

But I don't believe they have a right to know everything any more than the public does. Again: the Giants are private enterprise. Not Con Edison. I can't repeat that enough, either.

I don't read an awful lot of what is written about the Giants; I read enough to get a sense of the message the fans are getting about my team, though. Generally, the guys who cover the team and are trying to *cover* the fact that they don't know a whole hell of a lot about football, will immediately ask me statistical questions on Monday. They'll use stats to try and evaluate a player's performance.

With these guys, if Simms went six-for-eighteen the day before, then he has officially had a lousy game. They don't want to know about dropped balls, lousy patterns, receivers falling down, any of that.

He only completed a third of his pass attempts, so he must have stunk the joint out.

"So, uh, Simms had a bad game?"

Me: "You think so?"

A lot of times, the writers will get mad at me on Monday because I can't tell them as much as they'd like to know about the injuries. Actually, I'm not busting their balls there, because I haven't had a chance to sit down yet with the trainers.

Another thing I love is the Big Bang Theory of covering football games. For instance, if a defensive back gets beat deep, then he must have had a bad game too. It doesn't matter that there might be seventy-five or eighty plays in a game and this guy was pretty damn solid on the rest of them before one slip.

"So, uh, Elvis didn't look too good yesterday?"

Me: "You think so?"

Every play is supposed to be life and death. That comes more from the television commentary than the writers, except that a lot of the writers tape the game they're covering and go home and watch it afterward and then they start listening to what the announcers are saying, and what the announcers are saying begins to color the writers' opinions. It's a vicious circle, because I've got to level:

Not all those "experts" are Pat Summerall and John Madden (who are so clearly the best there's little to discuss). See, Summerall and Madden work their asses off when preparing for a telecast. They work the field, they work the locker room. It's like they're going to be coaching the game with me. They've done a lot of Giants games over the past few seasons and—I'm not kidding—they've come to know our team the way assistant coaches would, or coaches preparing to play *against* us. They sometimes hear a bunch of crap about how they're prejudiced in our favor. It's just that. Crap. They are total professionals.

But not everybody is, even though they stick them in blazers and give them microphones.

I hear more b.s. when I tape some games.

He shoulda passed more.

He shoulda called time out there.

Often, they don't have a *clue,* but don't ever think these guys aren't powerful as hell. You'd be amazed at how much of my mail about the team reflects the commentary, or what the press has written about the game, or both.

It doesn't mean that everybody is in a fog. For all the bad ones, you still have Maddens and Summeralls. They understand what happened on Sunday. They can see why that series or the next one was important. They understand why the momentum changed when it did. You don't have to draw them a picture. It's the same with writers. You can tell by the questions they ask that they have a feel for what's going on. If you want to know who I respect in the media, it's the ones who do their homework, who seem to me to be as relentless about their jobs as I am about mine. I know who those guys are, and I know who the fakes are, the ones who just aren't around and still pass themselves off as experts. I don't care whether guys are after positive information or negative information, as long as they're aggressively getting after the truth. (Though that has its limits too. Joe Morris ended up in the hospital this year after an allergic reaction to medication, and I got *extremely* irate when the boys thought it was all right to call the nurses' station and try to call Joe himself about twenty-five times a night. You think that's what they had in mind when they drew up the Constitution?) I know the guys who study the game, who truly work hard at their jobs, who do a good objective job of reporting no matter what their newspapers or radio stations tell them to do. And deep down in my heart, I'm always going to try to help out the guys who work the hardest.

Sorry, that's my nature.

You want to waste a lot of your time when you're supposed to be working? Fine, just don't expect me to waste a lot of mine.

I grew up in the New York/New Jersey area, and I feel like after all these years I know a little something about the newspaper business. And now being on my side of the tracks, I have a better feeling for how things are presented. I'm fascinated by what I do read about the Giants, because I can see the genesis of it from my own point of view, and I know what the real information is. Writers pool report, they surrogate report. I don't believe anything actually falls into the category of "off the record." The statement a player makes may be off the record when he first says it. But then the writer who was there might tell another writer. He'll think, I wasn't there, it wasn't off the record for me, so the information goes into the paper, with or without the player's name.

Now it's in the paper.

So the other guys think, hey, he wrote it so I better cover my ass and write it.

It doesn't happen a lot. But it happens. I really don't see a lot of it with our beat writers, most of whom I like (but not all). There's a couple I don't trust, but just a couple.

I tell them all the same thing: "You deal with me honestly and I'll do the best I can to deal with you honestly. But you try any of that cloak-and-dagger junk, and

I'm not going to say anything."

Occasionally, I'll have to remind my players of something important too.

Me: "I'm not going to make statements behind your back, I'm not going to make public statements about you, I'm not going to get at you by planting little stories in the newspaper. So if a member of the media comes up to you and says, 'Parcells says this about you,' well, don't believe it if you haven't heard me say it." Because there are people in the media who like to drive wedges between players and coaches, and sometimes it doesn't take much of a fissure and pretty soon you've got an entire fault going. Parcells said this, what do you want to say back? Coach, Joe Blow said this, do you care to respond?

If a press guy comes to me and says, "Bill, Joe Morris said this about you," you know what my reaction is? I say, "I didn't hear Joe Morris say that, okay? My reaction is that I don't have a reaction."

We don't have too much of a problem with that around the Giants. It comes up from time to time and I deal with it on the spot, but generally speaking, I don't mouth off about my players and my players don't mouth off about me.

There's so much that seems to go on with the newspaper business, especially with the New York papers. You've got a certain segment of society that's going to read the *Times,* a certain segment that's going to read the *Post* and the *Daily News.* I think there are social reasons for this and economic reasons, all sorts of reasons. And I'm not saying the *Daily News* is the same as the *Post* by any means, because it's not. But I'm aware that a couple of papers like that are competing for the same dollar. The competition is pretty heavy, I gather. So I'm not really surprised when somebody from a paper comes to me— this has happened—and says, "Bill, I don't like it, but my editor wants me to stir up some controversy." Honest to God. The writer will say, "My editor thinks things are going too good, everything's too nice and smooth."

So you get that. And you get these scare headlines that have nothing at all to do with the story underneath. *Nothing at all.* The headlines on the back page don't reflect content *or* context, sometimes they don't even reflect the true subject matter.

But I understand it all, and I try not to take any of it personally. If somebody wants to get on my ass about something, fine. The only thing I won't stand for is when it's obvious that a writer has a personal vendetta going with a player, the coach, the general manager. If the writer allows that to get in the way—*consistently* allows that to get in the way—then I think that is horseshit. Because then you're dealing with a blind man. His eyes are closed and so is his mind. No matter what happens of a positive nature, he can't suppress his bias. He can't hold back the one thing that makes him anti-Parcells, anti-Simms, anti-Mara. He can't suppress it and he has no chance in hell to be objective. Then he does a disservice to his profession, the people he works for, and certainly to the people involved. And the same goes for me. If I don't like a reporter personally and I'm busting his chops every day even though he's around every day trying to do his job, then I'm not being fair either.

Yeah, man. It's a fulltime job.

Sometimes you're a narc.

Sometimes you're Dr. Joyce.

And sometimes you've got to be a freaking journalism scholar.

There ought to be a school someplace coaches could go to.

While I'm on the field Monday for the short workout, the assistant coaches are inside starting to work on the scouting report for the next opponent.

You didn't think Monday was over, did you? Just because the players got to go home?

Hell no.

Before the coaches leave, they've got to have their part of the scouting report for the next opponent completed. And the opponent's statistics have to be updated, their offensive and defensive tendencies brought up to date. And all of that has to be left on the desk of our secretary, Kim Kolbe, to be typed up on Tuesday morning. We call Kim Kolbe "Midnight." She works late hours like everybody else. To me, she's as valuable a member of the coaching staff as anybody. She's my assistant in charge of keeping the coaches organized and trying to help keep the head coach from going insane. You ask any of my coaches. We couldn't make it without Midnight.

If we're lucky on a Monday, we get home in time to watch Monday Night Football at nine o'clock. So it's only a fifteen-hour day from leaving the house until you get back to the house. There have been times when we flew all night from the west coast after a game out there, landed about five a.m., and came straight to the office for the fifteen-hour day.

Believe me, everybody does it this way.

And the week is only beginning.

The only players we see on Tuesday are the injured players coming for treatment. For the players, Tuesday is a wound-licking day, physically and emotionally and mentally. Oh, we'll see a lot of guys around the stadium who don't have to get treatment, but basically Tuesday is their free day. Get away from football for a little bit. Relax. Re-introduce yourself to your wife. That sort of thing.

For the coaches, Tuesday is longer than Monday.

Tuesday starts at the same time—six a.m.—as Monday, but doesn't finish until eleven at night. The day, and night, are completely devoted to looking at film of the next opponent and making the game plan. The offensive coaches are together, the defensive coaches are together, the special teams coaches are together, and I'm just bouncing a little from meeting to meeting:

"I thought about this."

"Have you considered that?"

"Do you think *this* might work?"

Every Tuesday, we construct a building from the ground up, is what we do. And every Tuesday, the building is different. I have thoughts, my assistants have thought, I have objections, they have objections. It gets pretty lively.

While we're doing all this, Kim Kolbe is typing out

the scouting reports from the day before, because when we're finally done with the basic work of the game plan, *then* the coaches have to sit down and start preparing for the next day's practice. I'm not kidding when I say Kim is like a coach. Sometimes I think she gets more involved in the games than we do. And she really does understand the mentality of coaches. She sees the anxiety and the frustrations and the crises and the devastations of a bad loss, the elation—Kim sees all of that. She's dealing with all of us, working the same hours most of the time.

So by the time eleven o'clock comes around, we've got a game plan we think can work, and we know what we have to do at practice the next day, because practice will relate directly to the scouting reports and the game plan itself.

We go home. But we know that when we show up at six or six-thirty the next morning we're still going to have three hours before the players show up if something has occurred to one of us overnight, or if we've got some loose ends in the game plan that need taking care of.

At ten on Wednesday morning, I have a squad meeting, and it's there every week that I give my keynote address concerning Sunday's game. I'll talk generally about what I think we have to do on Sunday, go back over some of the things Monday that related to where we are in the season, explain what we'll be doing that day at practice, and why. Sometimes, this one gets a bit heavy. I don't hold back. I might single out a particular player at the Wednesday meeting. Or I'll challenge somebody.

I'll say, "Lawrence, you got to do better than you've been doing or we've got no chance of winning the damn game Sunday."

Or I'll say, "Leonard, it's time for you to pick it up, okay?"

There's no point in wasting time, and no point in *not* saying it in front of the team.

But on the flip side, I might toss a bouquet of roses at a guy who deserves them.

"Lawrence, that was your best game of the season Sunday."

"Leonard, I've never seen you attack the pass blocking any better than that."

I want them to know exactly what I'm thinking before we get to work on the game so they don't have to read it in the newspaper. Your players just have to constantly know where they are during the season. As a coach, it's your job to give them their bearings if you think they need them. It's the only shot you've got to stay on course. Where are we as a team? Where have we been? Where are we going? You better be the captain of your own *goddam* ship, and you better not get lost. Everything is context. The things you talk about early in the season don't apply necessarily in the middle of the season, and the things in the middle of the season don't apply to the stretch run.

The speech only lasts about fifteen minutes, but they better be absorbing it. If I've been talking about blitz pickup, they better have blitz pickup on their minds, because when we go out on the field, I don't want to have to be repeating myself. It's Wednesday. We're playing Sunday. Don't waste my time or your time. It could be blitz pickup, or the goal-line offense. Sometimes it's more than one thing. But they're paying attention. Monday was a soft day and Tuesday was nothing.

Wednesday, let's start getting our game faces on, boys.

That's a basic theme of the keynote too.

We break off after that meeting If we plan to work on two segments of special teams in practice—say, kickoff and kickoff return—they'll break off and have a meeting. Then the offense and defense get together and get their scouting reports and game plans. We eat lunch. The offense and defense do a little more film work, like a refresher course from Monday. By one-thirty we're usually on the field for a long, hard, intense practice that usually goes to about four. They come in from the field. Some of them lift weights. Some of them just shower and go home.

Coaches stay.

At 5:30, every day of the season, we have a staff meeting. The practice has been taped.

We watch the practice.

Every day.

Sometimes this is difficult on the coaches, because I make them watch it together. Did I maybe say some things during the keynote that the players didn't like? At the daily staff meeting, I'm going to say things that the coaches don't like. Hey, we are all in this together. You check sensitivity at the door.

Me: "Are you kidding me? Can't we do better than this on the damn blitz?"

"Hey, Pat, are we *ever* going to get this guy going?"

"Bill, I'm sorry, but this scheme doesn't look too good to me at all."

Watching this exciting rerun of practice usually takes ninety minutes or so, sometimes two hours if I've got a lot on my mind and I keep stopping it to point things out.

It's about seven-thirty by now.

And we're done, right?

Nope.

(You starting to reconsider that challenging career as a professional football coach?)

We've got to plan practice for *Thursday*. We can't plan practice for Thursday until we see what happened *Wednesday*. So we talk about what worked that day and what didn't work. What did we overlook? What do we want to repeat? (And if we do have to repeat things, which I don't like too much, we better get them right on Thursday, because they are damn well not going to be repeated again.)

Wednesday we probably worked on the basic parts of the game plan: middle-of-the-field offense, first-down offense and second-down and third-down for that part of the field. Thursday we're going to get a little more specific: We're going to work on the goal line. We're going to work short yardage. We're going to back up a little from the goal line and work on our inside-the-twenty offense.

If we're lucky, we all get home about nine Wednesday night.

Beats working, don't you think?

T hursday is a lot like Wednesday. Only it's getting closer to the game now, so mistakes are going to make the head coach *irate*. By the time we sit down for the staff meeting on Thursday and start looking at practice from that afternoon, well, if I'm going to lose my temper, I'm going to lose it then. It's a bad deal for the coaches, because it's generally the players I'm mad at, but the coaches have to hear it first. The players are going to hear it the next day, but it's never quite as...volatile the next day.

And I have to watch this. Because I have a bad temper. I can get volatile, believe me. Mistakes at that point in the week can make me just go off. If there is one thing I've got going for me in this area, it's that I don't carry a grudge. If I want to get something off my chest then I get it off my chest and it's over and done with. It's something I've worked on throughout my career. Maybe it's getting older. Maybe it's getting smarter. I've seen more things. I've got a better idea what works and what doesn't.

Still, Thursday is the beginning of anxiety time. I know what I expect from the other team on Sunday. And what I'm seeing on Wednesday and Thursday gives me a pretty clear picture of what I can expect from my team. So I want things to be right. I get more demanding as the week goes on. *Every* week. The players know, and like to joke about it to the assistants: "Coach is starting to get the tight ass on us."

They think this is very funny.

Sometimes I don't think they understand the gravity of the situation.

The meeting schedule for just about everything is the same on Friday, but now we're getting very specific about things. We're going to run our two-minute offense. And we're going to create what we call a "move the field" situation for our team. We're going to simulate about twenty or twenty-five plays of down-and-distance situations for our team. You know: We've got third-and-six on their thirty-five-yard line, what are we going to do from here on in? And we're going to practice substitutions on defense according to the down and where we are on the field, and substitutions on offense (second-and-twenty, we'll take out fullback Maurice Carthon, bring in wide receiver McConkey or something).

Friday is for *polishing*.

And we keep working on what I call a blitz review, on both sides of the line. The defense blitzes. The offense picks up the blitz. We work on this about three days a week with the Giants. I don't think you can ever work on it enough. It is mostly for the benefit of the quarterback. I want my quarterback to go into the game confident that our players know what to do against the pressure. I want him to have a feeling that we're going to find a way to block blitzes, that we're going to make the proper adjustments, from the guards and tackles to the receivers down the field.

Phil Simms—*any* quarterback—has to know that the people in front of him are going to be able to *function* under pressure. And that means blitz pressure. I don't see anybody in the league spending as much time on this as we do. I want Phil to be almost glad to see a blitz, because we've been working on it so diligently that he comes to look at the blitz as a terrific opportunity for him to throw the ball down the field and get us an easy touchdown.

Believe me, he's become great at that.

It's his own skill and toughness and resourcefulness, mind you. But I do think it goes back to the time we've put in, dating all the way back to July. We start then. We don't stop working on the blitz until the season is over.

Everybody gets tired of me saying it, but I keep saying it, from July on: "We've got to be ready in case they wholesale us."

If some team comes out and just tries to wholesale blitz us the entire game, just maintain it all the way through, I want us to be ready.

(We usually are.)

Saturdays are just for easing toward the game. That's if we're at home. If we're playing on the road, we generally travel on Saturday. If we're at home, the team comes in at nine-thirty in the morning. They get their rookie-supplied donuts. It's a Giants tradition, don't ask me when it started. The first-round draft choice has to bring orange juice and coffee and donuts for the whole team. The donuts are serious business, believe me. Eric Dorsey, our No. 1 out of Notre Dame last year, brought the wrong kind of donuts the first couple of weeks, and I nearly had a player revolt on my hands. So Carl Banks, who remembered where to go and what kind to buy when he had to buy the damn donuts, had to show Dorsey how.

No kidding.

Some players came up to me and said, "Bill, you've got to get Dorsey to shape up on this donut situation."

We're talking about *donuts* here.

Now, in addition to all my other skills, I'm that guy who runs all the cookie stores.

David. I'm "David's Cookies."

After the donuts we go through a light workout—no pads—maybe talk a little more about things I've been harping on during the week. We even talk a little bit about the officials. Hell, you've got to scout them the way we do the opposition. What kind of personality does this guy have? What kind of personality does that guy have? *He* likes to call this. That guy might be inclined a little more to let you get away with that. Watch out for *that* guy, he's got a temper like someone shooting up a flare, he'll put a flag on you so fast if you open your mouth it will make your head spin.

That sort of stuff.

Then we go home and watch college football and take it easy and get ready to try to beat somebody's ass on Sunday afternoon in what you call your National Football League.

Monday through Sunday.

Nothing to it.

Then show up on Monday morning at six and get right back on the merry-go-round.

I've never really thought I did anything particularly great during the 1986 season or in the Super Bowl.

No false modesty there.

Collectively—coaching staff and players—I thought we *all* did something great. You hear a lot about this guy or that guy in some sport being a genius as a coach or manager. Well, there aren't too many of them walking around that I know about. What you end up with a lot of times are combinations of excellent situations, the right blend of people, hard work, luck. *That's* what we had last season with the Giants.

And I hope we still have.

No one has a better staff than I do.

As I've mentioned, Ron Erhardt—old Fargo—is my offensive coordinator. I'll always have a special feeling for him, because it was Ron along with Ray Perkins who got me into the league. If he has one strength above all others, I think he has a real flair for developing the ground game. He's also done a tremendous job, in my mind, working with Phil Simms the last four years. Ron's had a lot to do with instilling confidence in Phil, and I think that confidence is reciprocal.

I've heard some stuff from time to time that I ought to hire a quarterback coach. Well, Ron Erhardt works with the quarterbacks and does a fine job, thank you very much.

My defensive coordinator is Bill Belichick. He is one of the bright, creative minds in professional football, all at the age of thirty-five. Bill has a lot he brings to the dance. His dad has been a coach at the Naval Academy for over thirty years. Bill himself graduated from Wesleyan University, and basically has been coaching ever since. I firmly believe he could be anything in the business world he wanted to be, from Wall Street guy to lawyer. He has one of those minds. But football is in his blood. He's been working in the NFL, starting with the Baltimore Colts, since he was twenty-two.

Bill was special teams coach when I came to the Giants as defensive coordinator. And we've worked well together ever since. He's got a quality I admire a lot in an assistant coach: He's never afraid to speak his mind. Bill Belichick, when it comes to his job, doesn't understand what it means to be afraid. In his job, you can't be afraid to attempt aggressiveness. When he sees something or thinks something, I am definitely going to hear about it. When it comes right down to it defensively, I'm a lot more conservative than he is. We've had some arguments over the years and some of them have been beauties, but Bill has been terrific for me and for the Giants, and there's no doubt in my mind he's going to be head coach somewhere, probably before he's forty.

Pat Hodgson is my receivers coach, and one of my favorite people. We go all the way back to Florida State. He's a Georgia guy, funny, gregarious, loyal, worker, keeps us all loose. He is also the most creative member of the staff when it comes to the passing game, and Ron and I both lean on him a lot. Do not let Pat Hodgson's manner fool you: He wants to beat those other guys in the worst way.

Mike Pope, who coaches the tight ends, is another guy I met at Florida State. He's another colleague who turned out to be a close friend. Is Mike Pope good? All you have to do is look at our tight ends. Zeke Mowatt was on his way to being an all-Pro when he hurt his knee in the last preseason game of 1985. Now Zeke has come back to be as talented an "other" tight end as there is in the game.

Most places he'd be first string all the way. The only problem with the Giants is that the fellow in front of him is named Mark Bavaro. He's another Pope masterpiece. If you watched any Giants game last season, you know all about Bavaro. Pretty soon, it's going to be hard to find anyone at his position better than Bavaro.

Fred Hoaglin is the perfect man to coach our offensive line. He was an offensive lineman—a center—in the NFL, and he identifies very strongly with offensive linemen as a result. He understands and appreciates their problems, can tell them all about the fact that they're going to get very little recognition. Fred has done a lot to unify our guys in the offensive line (Billy Ard, Chris God-frey, Bart Oates, Karl Nelson, Brad Benson) as a group, a unit. He never lets them divide. They're a five-man team.

Hoaglin is known as Fred Fog around the team. It's just because he's incredibly focused on the next oppo-nent, the next defense his guys have to face. The big joke around the Giants is that he really doesn't *know* who the next opponent is, just knows the defense.

"Who we playing this week, Fog?"

"Four-three."

"Come on, Fog. Tell us the name of the team we're playing."

"Under."

Great coach, Fred Fog. And some piece of work.

Romeo Crennel is our special teams coach, and a very special person, at least from my point of view. Ro-meo has taught me a lot just by being around. He's black, Romeo is, and when he looks out at the world, he is the most wonderfully color blind person I've ever met. He just wants to know who you are. He doesn't bring any ex-cess baggage or prejudices to evaluating you as a person. He has a good heart.

Romeo was assistant to Belichick with the special teams my first year with the Giants as defensive coordina-tor. Our first preseason game was with the Bears in Chi-cago. When it was over, he was positive he was going to get fired.

You have to understand, with the extra players around—it seems like a million of them on the sideline that first preseason game—the sideline can get extremely hectic. With a lot of these guys, you barely know the names, much less the numbers. And you're always running them in and out of the game pretty fast.

Anyway, the Bears blocked an extra point.

Ray Perkins came running down the sideline toward Romeo.

"Who blocked that?" Perk snapped.

Romeo wanted very badly to have the answer at that particular point in time. He didn't. He told Perk so in this real small voice.

"Well," Perk said, giving him one of those great stares, "You goddam well better find out." And walked away.

Romeo said, "I've really enjoyed my career in football. One preseason game."

Fortunately, he's still around. We have terrific special teams with the Giants and a kicking game that won us about three games on our way to the Super Bowl, and Romeo Crennel is a big reason. His assistant on the special teams is an ex-Marine named Mike Sweatman. There is just too much going on with the special teams for one man. Mike, who has the rare combination of heart and toughness, complements Romeo beautifully. The two of them don't miss a trick.

I'm just really lucky with assistants. Len Fontes has another thankless job, coaching the defensive backs, and he does damn well at it. Lenny's a street guy, tough guy, likes the pressure, and you better like it coaching the guys who are all alone back there, and take so much heat if we lose. For some reason, it's harder to find defensive backfield coaches than any other type of coach. So when you get a good one, you hold on to him. Fontes can take the heat. And I give him some.

Lamar Leachman is another beauty. He coaches our

defensive line. He's got this shock of white hair and looks like some grizzled character actor. He's the most vocal of all our coaches, the most demonstrative. He's just an old-fashioned *coach* is what he is. He was the line coach when I got here and he's still the line coach. With good reason. He will find out what a player's limit is, and just push him to it, and beyond it. You can go ahead and give Lamar Leachman a lot of credit for Jim Burt and Curtis Mc-Griff and Jerome Sally, guys like that, because Lamar just wouldn't let them be anything else except NFL players. He's from Cartersville, Georgia, and it's not like Cartersville has ever gotten out of that voice of his.

Ray Handley, one of the gentlemen of coaching, is in charge of our running backs. I go all the way back to West Point with Ray, and I hope he's always going to be around for me. He worked for me at Air Force. We were all set to be reunited at Stanford until Rod Dowhower quit Stanford and took the Broncos job in 1979. Ray knows a little something about the running game. He ought to. He was an all-American back at Stanford, and held most of the schools rushing records until Darrin Nelson came along. Once I survived the cut with the Giants and got things organized, you can bet I wanted Ray with me again. And when we finally gave him a combination like Maurice Carthon and Joe Morris to work with (with Lee Rouson and Tony Galbreath and George Adams and then Ottis Anderson as backups), Ray knew what to do with it. Around the Giants, no one can gang up waiting for the pass anymore.

So it's Ray, and Romeo, and Belichick. All of them. There are assistants to the assistants whose names I've left out. You know about the Giants players. You don't know a lot about my staff.

You see, my staff ought to be right there with me in the last minute of victories, when Harry Carson goes into his act.

Again: No false modesty. If I go through boot camp every week getting ready for these games, so do they. So they deserve to be under those Gatorade showers too.

Not that any sane man would want to be, of course.

19 •

One over

Par

We lost two games during the 1986
season.

One of them was my fault.

Dallas 31, Giants 28.

Hell, we went out and bogeyed the
first hole.

I knew the defense wasn't ready to
play the season. I had known for a month.
I hadn't done my job preparing them.

It happens.

I knew it after our first preseason
game in Atlanta. I told the defensive guys
that they didn't have it in gear. I knew it.
They knew it. Anybody who watched the
freaking game knew it.

I said to them, "You guys think you
can turn it on and off and you can't. It
doesn't work that way. There's a hell of a
lot of talent on this defense. Nobody would
deny that. But you SOB's aren't working

hard enough at your jobs right now."

It was a mistake.

I shouldn't have told them.

You say, "Why the hell not? It's your job, isn't it?"

No.

It's my job to know when to give them hell and when not to give them hell, and the first preseason game wasn't the time. Because the defense got its ass kicked in Atlanta. That was good. That was *excellent*. They weren't working hard enough, just like I told them, and they deserved to get their asses kicked. I should have let that happen a couple of more times before I opened my big mouth. If I had, I might not have *had* to open my big mouth. Damn, you don't do your Rockne with a month to go before the regular season. Atlanta had given my defense a better message than I could by beating us up. If I had let that go on for a while, it would have created a much greater sense of urgency as the season did approach. Instead, I have to go barging in there and tell them they can't turn it on and off anytime they want to.

But I don't think that's what they heard.

This is what I think they heard: "Guys, I really am pissed about what I saw in the game, I'm not faking it, but it's only a headache, let's take a couple of aspirin, fix it right now, and get on with things."

Dumb.

Because the speech *worked*. They went out and responded for the next couple of weeks, played a little better, and got it into their minds that everything was all better, when it wasn't. And when the season opened, they still weren't ready.

I could blame the opening game loss to the Cowboys

on the fact that Joe Morris—who'd walked out of training camp over a dispute about a contract he wanted renegotiated—didn't show up with the new contract signed until the afternoon of the Monday night game. I could tell you it threw all my preparation out of whack, that I didn't know if I was going to have my best runner for that game or for the season.

All of that was true.

But the offense didn't lose the opener, and neither did Joe Morris' lack of work. The defense lost the game. You can't play a team like the Dallas Cowboys and not be fully ready. Not when you're playing against Tony Dorsett and Herschel Walker and Danny White and Randy White and the rest of those guys. So those guys played better than we did that night. Our offense played well enough to win. Our defense didn't play nearly well enough to win. We couldn't stop the Cowboys in the last minute, and nobody on our team seemed to be able to tackle Mr. Herschel Walker all night long. With 1:16 left in the damn game, Herschel took a handoff from Danny White on a neat draw play and scored the touchdown that beat us.

If the game had gone two more quarters, the Cowboys probably would have beaten us 45–28 instead of 31–28.

I was not pleased.

I was not pleased at all.

Me: "I told you guys this was coming."

I was talking to the defense.

"But you didn't want to listen. Maybe you guys think you're the defending champions of the world. Well, go look it up. You're not. If you don't get your asses in gear, and I mean right now, it's going to be a very long year around this team."

I didn't yell. I don't even remember raising my voice.

I said, "It's right there in front of you. You play like you did tonight all the way through, and we're going to be lucky to win ten games."

When I was done, I went off by myself. Lawrence and Harry came and found me.

Lawrence said, "Don't worry, we're going to get this thing squared away among ourselves."

Harry said, "He's right. We've already talked about it among ourselves. We'll take care of it."

I wasn't so sure. In 1985, two of those close losses had been to the Dallas Cowboys. One was by a point. One was by a touchdown. So all of a sudden, we'd played one game in the new season and it looks a lot like the old season, and I didn't like that too much.

Going into the old season, I *thought* we might win it all.

Going into the new season, I felt like we were *supposed* to win it all.

There's a difference. I figured it was our time to stop winning one game in the damn playoffs, then going home.

I wanted to go to the Rose Bowl in January. And not to watch Michigan play UCLA or somebody.

I just liked the team a lot. I liked the mix of young and old. I liked the unity. I liked that even our stars weren't flashy guys. I liked our depth, everywhere except running back, where George Adams, backup to Morris, was out for the season. I wasn't sure about our place kicking, but we got that straightened out later when we signed Raul

Allegre. (If you don't have a good kicking game in the National Football League, don't even bother showing up. All it means is the difference in three or four or maybe even five games a season. If you don't think three or four wins is important, go check those standings at the end of the season and see who makes the playoffs and who doesn't and by how much.)

Bavaro, the quiet kid from Notre Dame, was ready to be a star at tight end, and Zeke had come back to be his trusty sidekick.

I had Simms and Morris.

I had Tony Galbreath, another one of our veteran gentlemen and a locker room leader, to come in on passing downs and catch the ball. Tony doesn't get a lot of ink, but there has never been *anyone* better in this league at coming out of the backfield, even when the other guys know he's going to do it, and catching the ball.

I had Lawrence back, and I had seen enough during training camp and the preseason games to know that I wasn't going to have to worry about Lawrence.

Banks was ready to be great, even if I had to tell him before the season, "I know you think you can match your own expectations for yourself, but that doesn't mean you're going to match mine. So make sure you match mine."

Harry Carson and Gary Reasons rounded out the linebacking corps. You don't hear a lot about Reasons. Hear this: He doesn't have to apologize to his fellow linebackers. Reasons is another one of the quieter Giants. He comes out of Texas by way of little Northwest Louisiana State. He is a big game player; in the 1984 playoff game against the 49ers, he intercepted Joe Montana twice. If there are adjustments to be made during a game, Reasons will make them, sometimes before he has to be told.

At defensive end, I had George Martin, playing like a kid again, enjoying our success like a kid. And he fit right in next to Burt, the free agent who'd by now made himself into one of the best nose tackles in the business. Burt's always been a kid inside about football.

On the other side of Burt was Leonard Marshall. Like Banks, he was ready for stardom. Leonard had come a long way from his rookie season, when he was fat, not working hard enough and basically didn't have a clue. It's funny: Leonard is really the biggest guy on the team and Joe Morris is the littlest at five-foot-seven, but their careers began to take off about the same time, during the second half of the 1984 season. In the 1984 playoff game against the Rams, Leonard made the most important defensive play of the game for us, stopping Dwayne Crutchfield on the goal line when the Rams tried to cross our defense up and *not* give the ball to Eric Dickerson.

Leonard Marshall is one of the most physically gifted players on the squad. I'm glad he didn't stay fat.

Then there was my favorite part of the team.

Offensive line.

I have more fun with them than with anyone else. Later in the 1986 season, after Joe Morris would get just thirteen yards rushing against the 49ers in our Monday night win, I would give them the nickname "Club 13." Just to goose them for the next game. I find it very challenging finding ways to goose them.

Godfrey and Benson. Ard and Nelson. Bart Oates at center. Godfrey and Oates had both come over from the

USFL. But it didn't take long for all of them to fit together. What they are mostly called is "The Suburbanites." I always see them in Oxford blue shirts and ties and carrying briefcases. Godfrey is a bit of an intellectual, with a wonderfully unusual mind (he is known as "Tunnel" to his teammates, because of the way he's always zeroing in on some new area of interest). Ard is a stockbroker in the offseason. Oates is a lawyer. Nelson's father is a stockbroker. Benson's got a car dealership for himself now, so he'll probably be showing up in a shirt and tie now too.

But by the beginning of the 1986 season, they had become as tough and consistent a blocking platoon as there is in pro football. They would never stop protecting Simms or opening holes for Morris. Nelson, the right tackle, and Bavaro, have had an awful lot to do with Joe Morris' success, because we run to their side most of the time.

Brad Benson? He has done more with his ability than any football player with whom I've come in contact.

That's all. The Suburbanites are my guys.

I had them. I had Lionel Manuel at wide receiver, ready to be a star until he got cut down in that fourth game of the season against the Saints. But that gave me an excuse—and a *need*—to bring back McConkey from Green Bay. If Dave Jennings was the toughest cut I ever had to make, McConkey was right behind. He brightened the locker room the moment he came back. He returned punts. He caught the ball. He blocked. He became the spokesman for the maligned receiving corps (one writer called them the "Blue Law" receivers, because he said they were never open on Sunday. They ended up showing the writer something, of course, the Sunday of Super Bowl XXI).

And, of course, McConkey said, "The grass is always greener my *ass.*"

The defensive backfield was solid, led by Hill, the ex-Raider, and safety Terry Kinard, a former No. 1 draft choice who had turned out to be something special. Kinard was my first No. 1 draft choice as head coach, and I probably scouted him more than I've ever scouted a player, because I wanted the pick to be *perfect.* Over the years, Kinard (who'd get hurt in the second Washington game in the regular season and be out the rest of the way) had made it perfect with his play. He's not real chatty, Terry isn't. I think it took him three meals we had together at Clemson before he talked to me.

He was back there with his pal, Perry Williams, who'd quietly developed into one of the better corners, and Elvis Patterson, who sometimes was one of the better corners and sometimes wasn't, but always kept things very lively.

(I'm not always crazy about lively. I'd rather not notice my defensive backs, because that means they're doing most things right. I tend to notice Elvis.)

It was a group ready to win. *I* certainly was ready to win. That Bears game hadn't been very far from my thoughts during the offseason. From January 5 on, I had been thinking and scheming about ways to get the Giants over the hump. I had weighed all the pluses and minuses and come up with a hell of a lot more pluses. What could have been a major problem—Lawrence's rehab—turned out to be no problem at all. And Joe signed his contract and decided not to sit out the season, like he'd been threatening.

Then came Dallas 31, New York 28, and we were 0–1.

20

That Championship Season

Coaches play them one at a time. But they do not think about them one at a time. The second game of the season was against the San Diego Chargers. All they'd done the week of their opener was score fifty points against the Miami Dolphins.

But after the Chargers, we had the Raiders in Los Angeles.

If the defense didn't play better, immediately, I thought we were staring at an 0-3 start.

We beat the Chargers, 20-7, at Giants Stadium. The game was a struggle. With ten minutes left, we still only led 10-7. Simms and Morris and the guys didn't put on the most memorable offensive display in the history of pro football. But the defense snapped to attention and made the old coach feel a little better. Not relieved. Just better. The guys intercepted San Diego quarterback Dan Fouts, one of the best there is, five times during one twenty-four minute stretch in the second half. It was one of those games that makes it look like Bill Belichick and the rest of the defensive coaches and I might have done something special that week in preparation. But with a team like San Diego that you don't play all that often—they're from the AFC West, of course—you need more than a boot-camp week. You don't just start getting ready the previous Monday. As I pointed out to the writers after the Chargers game, if you're in your right mind, you start getting ready in February.

It was not a perfect day. There aren't many during the regular season. Going in, you don't know when the injuries are going to come. You just know they're going to come. Against the Chargers, they came in a bunch, and to my three best wide receivers. Lionel Manuel went down with a neck injury. Bobby Johnson (he'd become maybe my best clutch receiver later on in the season) went down with an ankle, Stacy Robinson went down with a bad back. Pluses and minuses, all the time. The problems with the wide receivers caused by all these injuries wouldn't straighten themselves out until much later, and would be the reason Phil Simms took so much heat early on.

All in all, though, I made it more pluses than minuses, because we held the *San Diego Chargers* to a touchdown. We forced them into turnovers *every time* they had the ball in the second half.

In the locker room, I said to Peter King of *Newsday* (I call him "Relentless"), "Put away the funeral wreaths." This one really did go all the way back to February, and a brainstorm I shared with Dan Reeves. My defensive coaches went out to Denver and spent some time with Dan's coaches. Then John Mackovic (my old friend from West Point, head coach at the time with the Chiefs) sent his defensive staff to Giants Stadium for a few days. I think this sort of information-sharing was a little unusual, but Dan and I both thought it would help us a lot. His schedule called for games in the NFC East, something that only happens every three years or so. Our schedule had us playing San Diego, Los Angeles, Denver, Seattle during the regular season. You just don't learn enough from watching teams you don't see very often play in the preseason. And I had to play San Diego in the second week and the freaking Raiders the third week.

We beat the Raiders too. The Giants hadn't won a regular-season game on the West Coast since 1981. The Giants had *never* beaten the Raiders. My guys knew how I respected the whole Raiders program and tradition, if they didn't know how close I am with Al Davis.

Giants 14, Raiders 9.

After the game, I was about as excited as I can get. As we were running off the field, I gave Jim Burt a happy whack on the helmet from the blind side and nearly sacked him. And I said to Mark Bavaro, "We're on our way, baby, we're on our way."

In my mind, all wins are equal, but beating the Raiders was a little more equal. They were in the process of having the 0-3 start that I feared, but they were still the *Raiders*, you understand? They were Al's team. I didn't feel for a minute that I was showing him up or anything remotely like that. Playing against a friend's team is one of the hard parts of this job. But the team showed me something, and showed the Raiders something. This was the type of game the Raiders had been winning for years. They got you down in the dirt and then just whipped your ass because they were tougher than you. Well, it didn't happen this time at the Coliseum.

Joe Morris gained 110 yards, first time the Raiders had let somebody go over 100 in two years. Marcus Allen of the Raiders gained forty against our defense. It wasn't something you would have wanted to hang in an art museum, but we beat them all the ways we had to. "It was a war out there," I said afterward.

You bet. But we won.

Seasons are like games and games are like players, and sometimes they begin to pick up momentum. It was in the New Orleans game, fourth week of the season, that I began to notice that this particular Giants team had a definite aversion to losing.

The Saints at that point weren't the leanest, meanest opponent in the world, but we went completely to sleep early, and found ourselves down 17-0 early in the second quarter. This was the game Joe Morris missed because of an allergic reaction. Lionel Manuel would be lost until the playoffs when the Saints' Antonio Gibson cut his legs in the end zone and nearly busted his left knee.

And Bavaro had left the game with what I thought was a broken jaw, bleeding all over the place. When he left the field, with blood everywhere, Bavaro couldn't say anything.

Which was par for the course. Bavaro doesn't say too

much anyway. I've had some nice talks with him, and he answered a lot of questions for me about Eric Dorsey—they're both from Notre Dame—when I was thinking about drafting Dorsey. I think Bavaro's smart and funny. It's just that he's a "yup" and "nope" guy with the press.

In fact, he's become a legendary "yup" and "nope" guy with the press.

(When we had our victory celebration at Giants Stadium—after all that freaking nonsense about whether to hold the Giants victory parade in New York City or Jersey or the moon—the Giants who'd gone on to Hawaii for the Pro Bowl after the Broncos game had sent taped messages, to be shown on the message board. And they were all very nice, the guys talking about how proud they were about winning and how happy they were for the fans and so forth. Nice touch. But the biggest laugh and reaction and cheer came when Bavaro's mug showed up on the giant screen. This, as I recall, was Bavaro's touching and inspirational message to the fans: "Hi, I'm Mark Bavaro." Sort of gets you right here, doesn't it?)

Well, Bavaro didn't have much to say after he got his jaw looked at. But he came back into the game, he caught a touchdown and Zeke caught a touchdown. Raul Allegre, who we'd finally signed to be our place kicker, kicked a couple, and since it was his first game, I didn't know that our problems at that particular position were solved, and that Allegre would be damn near perfect the rest of the way.

We came back to win, 20-17. The year before, we couldn't take a punch. Now we could. Bavaro and everybody else. We found out afterward that the Giants hadn't come back to win from that big a deficit since 1970.

Harry Carson pretty much summed things up when he said, "I doubt we could have won this game last year."

He had that right.

What could easily have been a 1-3 record or even 0-4 was 3-1 instead. We were getting hammered a little on the ropes with body punches, but we were coming out swinging. The defense was carrying the offense a little, which meant things had turned around. The shock of not having Joe in there now had me officially thinking about the addition of a running back (it would turn out to be Ottis Anderson). Manuel being out set in motion the McConkey trade. But where a month ago I had been worrying about my defense, now I was worried about my offense.

Do not ever think a season is going to jump right off the drafting table and be what you thought it would be.

My bad dreams about the offense turned into authentic nightmares the next week. It was easily our worst offensive performance of the year. We won the game 13-6 against a bad Cardinals team, but we could easily have ended up in overtime if one of those marvelous instant replay calls had gone against us on what either was or was not a Cardinals touchdown.

It was a play in the corner of the end zone. Our Mark Collins defending against J.T. Smith of the Cardinals. We were leading 13-6 with about two minutes to play. Lomax threw. Collins tipped. The ball was in Smith's hands for a moment, but then clearly fell away as he hit the ground. The refs signalled incomplete.

But wait.

The dreaded "beep" came from the press box, which meant the play had to be reviewed by the damn Replay Official.

Shit. I did not feel any more secure because the man making the call in the press box was Art McNally, who is the head of all refs for the NFL.

I had come to hate the new rule. I'm for *anything* that will help officials officiate, but the delays had become ridiculous. The rule and the technology and the rest of that crap was supposed to help out with obvious calls, but if they're obvious calls, how come it was taking six or seven minutes sometimes for the eye in the sky to make his decision?

The decision was at least five minutes in coming. McConkey said later that when he used to play in the streets and there was a tough call, they didn't ask somebody to decide the issue from a second story window.

I said to the writers, "It was like waiting for a decision at a fight in Las Vegas with Don King the promoter and his guy the fighter."

Got a laugh.

I was only in a joking mood because we'd gotten the proper call and we'd won the game.

If we'd lost, I would have had to stop a whole gang of New York Giants from heading over to the officials' room and looking for the second-story man who'd made them go play an overtime.

The season was five weeks old and seemed like five years, but the SOB's were somehow 4-1.

Bob Knight came to the Eagles game at Giants Stadium. In his honor, the defense held the Eagles to just one field goal. We didn't want Knight to get cranky or anything with lousy defense. That was the day Lawrence told him not to throw chairs and Knight told him to go cover somebody.

Lawrence did. Everybody did.

The last loss of the season came the next week in Seattle. It wasn't our best game of the season, but we'd already stolen a few like it, so I wasn't ready to jump off any buildings. Simms actually had a chance to win it for us in the last couple of minutes. He threw a great pass to Solomon Miller, a rookie receiver I had to put in there, but the ball bounced off Miller's chest at the Seattle eight-yard line. Then Simms threw an interception and we lost.

The next Monday night—the night of the seventh game of the World Series—we began the twelve-game winning streak, the dream three months, when the Giants brought home the bacon. I have one big expression, one big theme, when it comes to sports: Winning is never final. You strive for it, you attain it if you're lucky, you savor it for a little while, then you get on to the next. Next game. Next season. Maybe even next championship. And as our streak grew last season, if you were around our players and in our locker room, you never saw much euphoria. You didn't hear a lot of big talk from our players. They would enjoy each win, chat about it with the press for a little bit, then start thinking about the next game. They had won regular season games before, and they had won one playoff game three different times in the 1980s. (That's why I've never gone for all that stuff about "long suffering Giants fans." Our fans are great and loyal and all that, but *long suffering?* We'd been giving them a pretty damn good product even before we won the Super Bowl. Players are long suffering, not fans.)

For the first time since I'd been head coach, I could see them keeping their eyes on the damn eagle. And one win brought another. And another.

And another.

On our way to the championship, we beat the Redskins three times. It may have been our proudest accomplishment of all. I think the Giants-Redskins rivalry epitomizes all that is good about the National Football League. It has tradition. Now it has two teams that have supplied a lot of excellence to the league in the 1980s. Both teams have their legends. I think we run a classy program. I think Joe Gibbs in Washington runs a classy program, in addition to being one of the finest coaches this league has ever seen. I admire the Redskins general manager Bobby Beathard, who seems to be able to retool his team in a hurry when things start to go wrong. The battles are always fierce between the two teams, and lately it seems like the division title is always hanging in the balance. Dexter Manley gets after Simms. Lawrence gets after Jay Schroeder, the Redskins quarterback. Brad Benson has fierce battles with Manley.

If you don't like the Giants vs. the damn Redskins, then pro football isn't your sport, pal.

What I'm saying is, it wasn't any cakewalk through Pasadena. Three wins over the Redskins. Two over the 49ers. Two over the Broncos. One over the Cowboys. There weren't any free passes around the board like you get in Monopoly.

There wasn't anything easy about it.

We'd go to 8-2 against the Eagles in Philadelphia. Giants 17, Eagles 14. It was the game when Simms went six-for-eighteen and nobody wanted to talk about dropped balls. The Giants fans had been booing him on and off all season—hell, they'd been doing it his whole career, often making him the fall guy for things that hadn't been his fault—and the receivers had been in and out of the lineup, and Manuel was gone and McConkey was back, and the passing game wasn't coming around, and everybody was saying, "Shit, the Giants are lucky they've got Joe Morris."

Before we went on the road to play the Vikings, I called Simms into my office.

"I don't want you to pay attention to anything that is written or anything that is said, because you are a great quarterback," I said.

Simms said, "I don't usually. Don't worry about me."

I said, "But I do worry. There's this suggestion that you haven't done this or you haven't done that, and all you've done the last three weeks is beat three tough, *tough* divisional opponents, the Cowboys and the Redskins and the Eagles. I know how hard it is for you not knowing who's going to be running down the field to catch the ball from week to week. I've seen the drops. But with all that, you've just got to remember one thing: You've got to go out there and continue to be the *daring* player you've always been. Hell with whatever's going on. Screw it. The only way you can keep being the great player I think you are is to be daring, every Sunday. Don't worry about the damn consequences. Be daring."

Daring, as you can see, was a theme of the day.

A few days later, Phil Simms completed the biggest single pass of our season.

It was more like he gave the whole team this great

kick in the butts and really got us going toward Super Bowl XXI.

There were seventy-two seconds left in the game against the Vikings in the Metrodome. The Vikings were leading, 20-19. Now understand: We were 8-2 and we'd been finding ways to win every week, but no one had given us any loving cups, and we were still life-and-death with the Redskins to see who was going to win the NFC East and get the home field if we had to play each other in the playoffs. And we were still life-and-death with the Bears to see which one of us would have the best record, in case we had to play *them* in the championship game.

(You play them one at a time, but you don't think about them one at a time, remember?)

So there we were, down a point, time running out, fourth down at our own forty-eight-yard line, seventeen yards to go, eight men in the Vikings defensive secondary.

If you are a Giants fan, and you were watching on television, and you've never thought Simms was the second coming of Chuckin' Charlie Conerly or Y.A. Tittle or Fran Tarkenton (all those ghosts Phil has always had to go up against), you didn't exactly love our chances.

Hell, *I* didn't love our chances, and I'm the guy who'd given Simms the pep talk about daring a few days before. It wasn't because I didn't have confidence in him, because I did. I'd meant everything I said to him in my office. But fourth down is fourth down, and on a play like that, you reach into the playbook and roll the dice and hold your breath.

Simms dropped back, looked around until the last possible second, threw the ball, got whacked, went down.

And completed it to Bobby Johnson for twenty-two

yards to the Vikings thirty-yard line. We moved into position and Raul Allegre kicked his fifth field goal of the game and we won, 22-20.

(Allegre had come in for a tryout earlier in the season. We loved his leg. There was a disagreement about his contract. I said, "Disagreement? The SOB is out of work. Disagreement. Tell him to pack his shit and get out of here." He did. Then he wrote me a letter and said that the whole thing about the contract was a misunderstanding.

I called Allegre up and said, "If you want to kick instead of negotiate, the job is yours. But I don't want any more misunderstandings." We got along fine after that, and I came to find out that when it came to kicking the ball through the uprights in the heat, Raul Allegre was tough as a freaking gladiator.)

I didn't hear a peep from anybody about Phil Simms, quarterback, lacking the necessities for greatness the rest of the season.

Didn't hear much after the Super Bowl, either.

The week after the Vikings game, Simms did it again against the Broncos. In the last two minutes, he completed a third-and-twenty-one pass to Johnson for a first down, then he hit McConkey for forty-six yards and Allegre came in and did it again. If Simms hadn't completed the pass to Johnson, there would have been no pass to McConkey and we would have had to punt the ball and Elway would have figured out a way to beat us, no doubt in my mind.

But Simms, daring QB, did it.

Magic time.

The regular season ended this way:

1) We played the first of two perfect third quarters we would play (the second, of course, came against the Broncos in Pasadena). It was the Monday night game against the 49ers. In San Francisco. At Candlestick Park, the same place where we'd lost two very tough playoff games in the 1980s. There was still a lot of blood in the joint.

By halftime of the Monday night game, there was a lot more.

Joe Montana 17, Giants 0.

We came back and won 21-17.

Hello.

In the third quarter, the Giants were just incredible. No other way to describe it. No other word necessary. Simms threw a touchdown pass to Morris. Simms threw a thirty-four-yard touchdown pass to Stacy Robinson. After Robinson made a circus catch on a bomb from Simms, Ottis Anderson ran it in from the one.

If Mark Bavaro hadn't fumbled at the six with forty-one seconds left in the quarter, we would have scored again. If there were still any doubts that 1985 was like another era for these Giants, they had erased them. The year before, we had lost our six games this way: three points, one, five, two, two, seven.

With the comeback against the 49ers, we had now won games, in succession, by seven points, three, two, two, three, four.

What is that? A difference of forty-one points across twelve football games. Yes, forty-one points. Six touchdowns and extra points, if you want to look at it that way. And those points, from one season to the next, made all the difference in the world.

Those forty-one points in twelve games were the difference between also-rans and champions.

2) Nice schedule. 49ers on the road on Monday night, Redskins on the road, Sunday afternoon. As it turned out, this was also our little playoff preview: First the 49ers, then the Redskins, just like the hand would be played in January.

No problem.

Giants 24, Redskins 14.

Afterward, Lawrence Taylor said, "I believe we're destined to do something great."

Peter King wrote in *Newsday,* "It is now permissible and altogether proper to talk about what a marvelous team the Giants have."

I thought it was permissible and altogether proper to talk about what a marvelous comeback Lawrence Taylor had made from the drug treatment and subsequent media bullshit.

Because he was magnificent against the Redskins. He was everywhere. This was the Lawrence we had seen come out of North Carolina, flying, one-handing the quarterback, dismissing blockers, coming at you from this side, then that side, never letting the offense get set. He looked *free.* He was the old Lawrence. It wasn't like he had been asleep the rest of the regular season, but this was a game out of his brilliant past. He was LT again.

Afterward, he opened up with the press for the first time. He had given the odd interview here and there, but this day in Washington it was like talking to the press was a way to extend his great day. He wanted to revel in it a little more. He smiled the whole time; he was talking in the middle of the locker room. The Redskins game had done a lot for us. If we beat the Cardinals the next week at home, we'd finally have won the NFC East, the first title of any kind for the Giants since 1963. And that was important, because I felt we should have won the division the year before.

And the Redskins game had taken something from us in the person of Terry Kinard.

But mostly, it was like a coming-out party for Lawrence.

The man can make the game look like a *game* sometimes.

3) We did beat St. Louis and win the division. When we took the field that day at Giants Stadium, I'd never heard a sound quite like it. Our home crowds are *always* loud, mind you. They make it awfully tough to beat us at home. There are no better fans.

But these cheers were different. It was happiness and relief and all those years of not winning any titles of any kind wrapped up into this one loud package. They knew we were going to beat the Cardinals, so did the players.

We did.

4) Giants 55, Packers 24.

We clinched the home field advantage for as long as we were alive in the playoffs. We had the same 14-2 record as the Bears, but we got the home field because we had only one loss—the Cowboys—in our conference. This time, if we won that first playoff game, we'd stay home.

We weren't going to San Francisco, and we weren't going to Chicago or Washington if it came to that.

I liked that very much.

There was but one team in the National Football League that had gone undefeated at home in 1986.

Us.

We had won more regular games than any Giants team in history. It was sixty-two years of history at that point. After all the struggling we had done on offense all season, we had scored fifty-five points against the Packers, the third-highest point total in Giants history. Other than Kinard, we were healthy.

And we were two wins away from Pasadena.

I was with Ernie Banks at that point.

Let's play two.

21

Uh, 66–3

It does not take very long for me to get from the house I grew up in at 109 Columbus Avenue in Hasbrouck Heights—across from the ballfield bracketed by Curtis Wright Aviation and Bendix—to Giants Stadium. I know. I've gone back there just for fun, then made the ride to my office at Giants Stadium.

My father grew up at 261 State Street in Hackensack. Another trip to the ballpark that is a piece of cake.

The closest of all is the house my mother grew up in at 57 Columbia Avenue in Woodridge. You just go down to the bottom of the hill from where the Naclerio's lived and then you get on Route 17 south and you take that over to Patterson Plank Road and you go east on Patterson Plank Road, and you're at Giants Stadium in five minutes if the traffic is good. Driver and a 9-iron.

The house we live in now? Little longer trip, but not too bad.

I know the area. It was the first part of my life, and it's my life again. Maybe I don't understand all the frustrations of Giants fans. The Giants were great when I left. Now they're pretty good again. I wasn't around in the '60s and '70s. It's sort of funny. Other than the strike year in 1982, I've only really known that one losing season—you remember, 3–12–1, right out of the chutes—in my own relationship with the Giants. When I went off to college at Wichita State, the Giants had just played a couple of championship games against the Colts.

Since I've been back, the Giants have been in the playoffs four times in this decade.

I look at things as they are now and, for me, they're like they always were.

Of course, they weren't. There were hard, mean years for the two owners, Well and Tim Mara. I've never talked to either one of them about those years. I'm not a big history buff when it comes to events that preceded me with the Giants. I don't know a whole hell of a lot about how George Young came to be hired in 1979. It's not like when I became head coach I went to one of the local newspapers and asked to see all the clips on this big feud that Well and Tim Mara are supposed to have, and how it got resolved long enough to get Young hired.

I'm sensitive enough to know that the Giants are Well Mara's whole life, have been his whole life. He's at the office every day, he's at practice every day, he loves hanging around the locker room and getting to know the players. He loves the life. I assume he's always loved the life. We don't have a lot of personal contact. We say hello and nod at the office, he's always in the locker room after games, win or lose. My take on him is that he's moral, devoted to his family and the Giants in that order, and that he is part of the real tradition of the National Football League, along with people like the Rooneys in Pittsburgh. They go all the way back: Well Mara's father, Tim, bought the team in 1925, and the Maras have owned it ever since and, I suspect, will always own it. George Steinbrenner was asked one time if he would ever sell the New York Yankees and Steinbrenner said, "If you own the Mona Lisa, you don't *sell* the damn thing." Well Mara, I'm sure, feels that way about the Giants.

I don't know how Well felt about me after the 1983 season, when it looked like the axe might fall. George Young is the buffer between the Maras and me on matters like that. All I know is that I got the new contract after the 1984 season. And no one has ever fought me on the expense of the weight room or paying the expenses for the players on the offseason program. My sense is that everyone down the hall (where the owners' offices are) has had more confidence in me as time has passed about personnel matters, things like that.

I don't believe the Maras are cheap. I think they— through George—aggressively tried to sign Joe Morris before his holdout last summer and honestly felt he should honor the contract he had for last season. I don't have any problem with them on money.

I'm aware the co-owners don't like each other, but it doesn't affect me. I'll see them pass without talking, but it's frankly none of my business. I didn't feel too comfortable when I first became head coach, because I'd heard this and that about the so-called "War Between the Maras."

And it has nothing to do with me. It does not filter down to the football operation. If there are disagreements between Well and Tim, and I'm sure there are, they have no bearing on the way I do my job. The only time I've ever gotten involved in their end of the business, to tell the truth, was when I suggested to Tim (he's Wellington Mara's nephew, son of Well's late brother Jack) that he spend a little more time around the team. I thought it was important to the players to know that both owners had a real interest in what we were doing.

Again: You do the best you can to create the proper environment.

I said to Tim, "I think it's important that you start coming to practice, and I think it's good for the players to see that you're a part of this thing too. You've got to be visible too."

And now he's done that, and he's found that he really likes coming to practice, being around. He's not there every day, but nobody said anything about him being around every day. I wasn't playing one co-owner off against the other. They both want to win. Maybe it's because Tim and I are closer to being the same age, but over the years, I've just gotten to know him better. He's been a big help to me just by being around because, again, I think it unifies the organization in the eyes of the players.

The players can read too.

The players hear things.

The older guys know the history.

So with both owners being around, I think it at least gives a little sense that, "Hey, we're all in this together, even if we have differences."

Well and Tim Mara don't love each other? Neither do George Young and Bill Parcells. But everybody wants to win, and that's the bottom line. When I ask for things that are important—Ottis Anderson, despite a fat contract—I don't get turned down. That cheap stuff really is bullshit. The Maras support the coach. They put out the money. They keep me out of their problems with each other. I can't ask for more than that.

And I don't think any of us could have asked for anything more than the last two Giants Stadium Sundays of our championship season. The rest of the adventure after that would be for southern California.

But before we left, we had a couple of Jersey days Giants fans had been waiting for for a long time. We finally showed Jersey what it used to be like at Giants Stadium when it was Conerly and Gifford and Robustelli.

The Giants became *giants* again.

Giants 49, 49ers 3. You ever have this perfect day in your life? You know, things sort of started breaking right first thing in the morning and they stayed that way all day long?

My guys had a perfect day against the 49ers. Bill Walsh, the 49ers coach, said afterward, "We were shattered by a great team."

We didn't look bad.

The 49ers turned the ball over to us four times. We scored a touchdown every time. Phil Simms only completed nine passes, and once again the stat sheet was misleading, because four of those passes were for touchdowns, and Simms looked outstanding when he had to. He threw one touchdown pass to Bavaro, one to Zeke, one to Johnson, one to his pal McConkey.

Joe Morris gained 159 yards.

The only thing that marked up the day for us was seeing Joe Montana of the 49ers leave the game on a stretcher and end up at the hospital for a CAT scan. Jim Burt game him a clean hit right before the half, as Montana was throwing the ball. This was the same Montana who'd made almost a miraculous recovery from back surgery earlier in the season; he not only wasn't supposed to come back and lead the 49ers to the playoffs, a lot of people thought his career was over. But as soon as Burt hit him, his season *was* over.

Burt, who'd overcome terrible back problems himself, wasn't too happy about it. He said he looked down at Montana and felt sick. He'd also say afterward, "It was like I ran right through him, Bill."

Lawrence, meanwhile, was running toward the end zone, because he'd intercepted Montana's last pass of the season. Lawrence didn't have time to think about Montana.

Lawrence said, "I was just thinking, 'Don't drop the SOB.'" His score made it 28–3 at halftime.

Strange game. I felt a drop by 49ers receiver Jerry Rice on the fourth play of the game might have taken the air out of the 49ers balloon. They had come in here the year before and not scored a touchdown. Now Rice breaks wide open for a sure touchdown and Montana tucks the ball in there.

Rice drops it.

Everybody thought I was crazy afterward, but I

thought Rice dropping that ball was like Landeta whiffing that punt the year before in Chicago.

If the Bears hadn't gotten a gift touchdown there...

If the 49ers had scored on Montana-to-Rice...

Like I said, people thought I was crazy. In the locker room, somebody reminded me of that 73–0 championship game the Bears had won from the Redskins back in the 1930s. That day, Redskins quarterback Sammy Baugh had a sure touchdown pass dropped on *him* early in the game. And afterward, Baugh was asked if things might have been different if the ball had been caught.

Slingin' Sammy Baugh said, "Yeah, we would have lost 73–7."

Whatever.

It turned out to be the toughest wind I'd ever seen at Giants Stadium. The gusts ended up at 32 mph by the second half, and the wind chill factor made the temperature sixteen degrees, and that was all right with the New York Giants because we beat the Redskins for the third time, 17–0 this time, and we were going to the Super Bowl to play the Broncos in two weeks.

Four years and one month from when I'd become head coach, we were all going to the big show.

The wind at Giants Stadium helped push us the last bit of distance to the NFC championship. Maybe the wind had been picking up momentum for a long time. One of the writers wrote the next day, "The wind was 30 *years* per hour" by the end of the game.

Maybe.

I'd been expecting to play the Redskins again all

along. Some people acted surprised that they went into Chicago the week before and beat the Bears, but not me. The Bears had lost Jim McMahon at quarterback, and Doug Flutie was asked to step right into the NFL and lead them to another Super Bowl, and I felt that was an awful lot to ask of the kid. Besides, I knew how good the *Redskins'* defense was while everybody kept talking about the Bears'.

So even though we'd beaten the Redskins twice, I was worried. You always worry when you play a Joe Gibbs' team. I've already said I think he's one of the best. I think he belongs in a category with myself and Dan Reeves and Bill Walsh and Mike Ditka and Tom Flores in what I call the "Ford" division. (I wouldn't have put myself in that group until the Giants won the Super Bowl, but now...what the hell, right?) I think we're all about the same.

There is, of course, a "Cadillac" division. Don Shula and Tom Landry are the Cadillac division of active coaches. Just the two of them.

I mean, I just couldn't think of comparing myself to either of them, or what they've already done in their careers.

So it was Gibbs and the Redskins again, anyway. And it turned out to be a game where the coin tosses and the decisions about whether to kick off or receive and what goal you wanted to defend turned out to be a big part of the story.

It doesn't make me a genius, because everybody could see and feel and *hear* the wind. I'd been calling the recorded number at Newark Airport and everywhere else for weather information from eight o'clock in the morning on. Now it was time for the four o'clock kickoff and the wind just kept picking up steam.

I told Harry Carson to take the wind, not the ball, if we won the toss.

We won the toss.

We took the wind.

Perfect.

Curtis Jordan, the Redskins safety, was a player I'd coached in college (Texas Tech), and one I'd always been quite fond of, because he was another guy I felt had done the absolute most with the ability he'd been given. After the game, he said, "The coin toss was as big as any play in the game."

Maybe.

After ten minutes we led 10–0. We started our first quarter drives at the Washington forty-seven-, the Washington thirty-eight- and our own thirty-nine-yard line. So it was 10–0. The Redskins had one big chance to do something in the first quarter but Gary Clark, wide open, dropped a long one from Jay Schroeder. Just like Rice had dropped the ball the week before. It stayed 10–0, same as it was at the half.

At the start of the second half, Washington chose to defend the goal with the wind. It was their choice, and they did what we'd done at the start.

But I chose to kick off, instead of take the ball.

Huh?

Here was the old coach's thinking on that one, because we'd never done anything like it before, have the option of the ball and kick off like that:

I figured that if we received, they'd kick it into the end zone, we'd start out on our twenty-yard line. We're not going to do anything tricky on the first series, so we're going to end up punting from about our five-yard line into the gale. Landeta, even with his leg, is going to kick it no further than midfield, if he can do that. So they're going to start their first drive of the second half at least on the fifty-yard line, and most likely deeper into our territory than that. But if we kick off, they're going to start out their first possession on their thirty-five-yard line, maybe less than that. They'd have sixty-five yards to go for a touchdown, instead of forty-five, or forty. If we could keep them on their side of midfield for one possession, I felt the third quarter was going to be a hell of a lot more even after that.

I felt the momentum of the game was all in our favor at that point. If our defense could hold the Redskins for the rest of the quarter, then *we'd* have the wind in the fourth, and then it would be lights-out time.

I wasn't sure of a lot of things in this world, but I knew this: With fifteen minutes to go and the Super Bowl staring at us and all those noisy Giants fans, the Giants weren't going to blow the lead.

Not with that thirty year per hour wind at our backs.

It worked out just that way. I had listened to the Giants win over the Bears in 1956 on my Bendix radio. This time, I was at the ballgame. It was freezing cold by the end of the game, and people were probably afraid that the Gatorade shower would turn me into the world's biggest ice sculpture, but I didn't care. After thirty years, the wind finally seemed to be at the Giants backs.

George Martin, I think, spoke for everyone when it was over. At least for us older guys who knew a little something about what had come before.

George said, "I keep expecting to wake up and be 3–12–1."

22

Twelfth Win in a Row

Everybody thought I made some big speech at halftime of Super Bowl XXI. We went into the locker room losing 10-9 and by the time the third quarter was over it was 26-10 Giants, and it was going to take the United States freaking Marines to keep us from walking off into the sunset with the Vince Lombardi Trophy.

So everybody just assumed that I stood up in front of the team and did my big number.

I didn't.

Now there have been halftime speeches of mine that have gotten fairly lively. Those are the ones that usually begin, "Maybe it's time to sew up our skirts, girls." The players generally settle in when one starts out like that, because they know it's going to be a dilly.

I didn't think at halftime, despite the

fact that we were losing, it was "sew up the skirts" time.

I said, "I don't mind losing the game, but let's not *give* the damn thing away, okay?"

I went on.

"I just don't think we played very goddam well out there. We're not playing well as a team, so that means offense, defense, everybody. But particularly the defense. Shit, you're just out there running around. You're not pressuring the quarterback, you're giving stupid penalties [Harry got a late hit, Lawrence yapped at the official and got one for unsportsmanlike conduct]. Like I said, let's not just hand them the sonofabitch. And so far, we're acting like that's what we're trying to do. I'll tell you guys the truth, I feel this way and you ought to feel this way: We're pretty goddam lucky that the game is about where it is right now. Considering the way we played, I think we should be freaking *delighted* we're only down a point. I'm not bitching about effort, I'm bitching about the way we're going about things out there. We need more discipline out there. I don't care how good some of you guys are, you can't do it *alone*. It's got to be a damn collective effort. Elway's gonna keep spreading the freaking field on you, and if you're not willing to play good, disciplined, aggressive team defense, we're going to blow everything we've worked for. The offense is going to move the ball in the second half. We haven't moved it great so far, but we've moved it fair. But the offense can't do shit if it doesn't have the ball."

It occurred to me that the whole thing had come full circle, because I was talking to the defense the way I had after the first preseason game in Atlanta.

If the first preseason game wasn't the proper time to

give them the talking-to, I thought this was.

"You're lucky you're in it," I said. "Now go win it."

We were lucky as *hell* we were in it. A lot of things had gone our way, and that's why what we saw on the scoreboard was still workable. On the first Denver drive, the Broncos got a field goal, but they might have gotten a touchdown if Kenny Hill hadn't remembered to count our players on the field goal defense. It was fourth-and-two for the Broncos from our thirty-one-yard line. A penalty for too many men on the field would have given them a first down, and the drive would have continued.

But Kenny, who studied molecular biophysics at Yale, also learned how to count there. When he got to eleven and was still counting, he called time out. Greg Lasker, a backup safety, thought he was supposed to be out there and he wasn't. I thought, Wonderful. But the Broncos only got a three.

Later on, with Denver leading 10-7, we made some luck and then got more. It was the second quarter. They had first-and-goal at our one-yard line.

On first down, Elway sprinted out to his right with a pass-run option. Lawrence Taylor sprinted right with him, and stuffed him for a yard loss. It was simply a great play by a great player.

Second-and-goal, from the two-yard line.

The Broncos ran Gerald Willhite up the middle. Harry Carson was waiting for him. *Everybody* was waiting for him. No gain. Zip. Nothing.

Third-and-goal. I'm watching from the sideline and thinking at the time that it might be the most important play of the game. If they score, they go up 17-7, and we're not playing too well, and maybe if they get a couple of breaks—hell, *one* break—we're down 24-7 at the half. And I don't remember anybody coming from 24-7 down to win what you call your Super Bowl.

Third-and-goal, anyway.

The Broncos ran Sammy Winder wide to the left. And then here came Carl Banks, the LT trainee, making as great a play as Lawrence did on first down, nailing Winder for a loss back to the six-yard line.

All season long—for a few seasons—we had been hearing about how wonderful my linebackers were. Now they were faced with first-and-goal from the one-yard line in the Super Bowl, and they were trying not to fall 17-7 behind, and this is how it went:

Lawrence on first down.

Harry on second down.

Carl Banks on third down.

On fourth down, Rich Karlis, the Denver kicker, missed a twenty-three-yard field goal. They had a chance to grab us by the throat, and they came away with nothing.

More luck: We punted after the missed field goal. Denver ball. Elway is at his twelve-yard line, but he throws the ball up the middle to Clarence Kay. At first, I thought Kay caught it. Then they signalled incomplete. Then the Replay Official in the booth looked at the replay pictures he was given, and the pictures were inconclusive, and the call stood. As it turned out, about nine minutes later, CBS came up with a picture that made it look like Kay indeed may have caught the ball, but by then it was too late.

George Martin had busted in on Elway on the very next play and sacked him for a safety, to make it 10-9.

Denver can "if" itself to death on that one, because if Kay's play had been called a catch, then Elway wouldn't have had to drop back into his end zone to throw, and if he didn't, George's sack wouldn't have have been a safety, and...

Whatever. The score was 10-9, and stayed 10-9 until halftime.

Then came the second perfect third quarter of the season, as good as the one against the 49ers in that Monday night game. It was the one that slammed the door on the Broncos. This one went all the way back to training camp, all that sweat, when the season began to take shape. This was the one you dream about if you're a coach. Because everything worked. All cylinders were clicking, on the biggest stage any of us had ever had. It was a close game, then it wasn't. Elway was making our defense look ragged, then he wasn't. Our defense wasn't playing together, then it was. And Simms? He fit very nicely into the perfect mode. He didn't throw an incompletion the second half of the Super Bowl. He went on to finish twenty-two-for-twenty-five. He got the MVP award for the game, and got the recognition he'd waited his whole career for, as one of the premier quarterbacks in the game.

On our first series of the third quarter, Jeff Rutledge ran his sneak, then Simms finished the drive with a touchdown pass to Bavaro. On our second series, Allegre kicked a field goal. On our third series, on a trick, flea flicker play, Simms took a lateral and threw one forty-four yards to McConkey, who helicoptered a bit (fitting, right?) after he got hit, and landed about two feet from the goal line. Joe Morris ran it in from there. It was 26-10.

You could have put a knife in the ball right there.

By then, the defense must have sounded like the ocean to the Broncos. They did not make a first down in the third quarter. They gained a total of two yards. We gained two hundred. Elway completed two passes. The last play of the quarter was almost symbolic. Leonard Marshall sacked Elway for a loss of eleven yards, and Elway fumbled. He'd recover it himself. Didn't matter. On the first play of the fourth quarter, Elway threw and Elvis Patterson intercepted. Giving the ball back to Simms at that point was like giving him a gun. He threw one for thirty-six yards to Stacy Robinson. Then it looked like he'd hit Bavaro for another touchdown and it bounced off Bavaro and McConkey caught it for the score and became probably the happiest man to score a touchdown in the history of the Super Bowl.

It was 33-13.

We'd scored twenty-four points in about nineteen minutes.

A few minutes later, after the Broncos had gotten a field goal, I became aware that our defense was celebrating already on the sideline. I went down and yelled at them. Hell, you've got to stay in character all the way through.

"Don't you guys start the goddam victory party until the goddam game is over!" They all looked at me like I'd lost my mind.

Because we all knew it was over.

I tried to stay busy until the end. The last five minutes seemed to take five hours. Or five years. I thought, couldn't we play running time, just this once? There was celebrating going on, I could feel it behind me. I didn't turn around. Let them go. I kept my eyes trained on the field, and tried to get everyone into the game. Ottis Anderson scored our last touchdown, and I was happy for him, because he'd never gotten near a Super Bowl during his years with the Cardinals, years when he was always one of the best runners in the game. He'd always been a winner on losing teams, but now it was official for him. Now he'd have a ring.

I thought about Al watching the game. I knew Knight was home watching it in Indiana; he'd talked about maybe flying in the day of the game, but Indiana had played Minnesota the night before, and it was just too much.

I thought about Mickey.

Chubby and Ida.

My wife and daughters.

I couldn't help my mind from wandering. I kept thinking about Hastings more than anything else at the end. I went all the way back there, and I thought about how relative everything is. It was still football. It was still a game. They could change the stakes on you. They could put you in a setting like this. They could make it a glitzy show for millions.

And it just went back to being football. How to get the sides even, like Mickey used to say, then go from there. How to beat them other guys, no matter who the other guys were. It could be New York vs. Denver. Hastings vs. Nebraska Wesleyan.

Was there elation? You bet.

But don't you always feel great when you win? How do you measure the levels of elation exactly? Like I say, it's never final. Every time you do it, you want to do it again. I guess maybe that's what keeps a Shula going, a Landry.

I'm sure that's what kept Coach Lombardi—now *he* was a Rolls Royce—going.

I thought about a lot of things. Wherever Perk was watching, I hoped he was happy for me, because I don't know how the whole thing would have played out if he didn't give me one chance, then another.

Finally, the clock ran out. The scoreboard at the Rose Bowl said that we had 39 points and that the Broncos only had 20.

Damn.

I was pretty wet by the time the gun sounded. They'd given me a double this time. Harry got me first with Gatorade, then his backup troops got me with a bucket of ice water. So if I was crying, I ask you: Who the hell could tell?

I knew the dressing room was going to be jammed as soon as we opened the door. I knew I wasn't going to have much time before there was all the business of the presentation of the Lombardi Trophy for television. So we all pushed together in the middle of the room, and some of us knelt and some of us didn't for a team prayer.

I just said, "No matter what anybody tells you the rest of your life, nobody can tell you you couldn't do it. Because you did it. They can't ever take that away from you."

Then all hell broke loose and the whole world seemed to end up in the little maid-closet locker room of the world champion New York Giants.

Pete Rozelle presented the trophy to Wellington Mara, as Well is president of the team. Well said, "I'm very proud to represent a great bunch of men, our coaches, and our players."

Brent Musburger of CBS stuck a mike in my face and said, "Can you do it again?"

What? He's got to know *now?* I wanted to punch him in the face, but I was polite and then he asked me about Phil Simms, which I thought was a little more appropriate, and I told him Simms had been "Magnificent." Then I went down into the mess of my guys hugging and kissing and tried to get to as many of them as possible and say thanks.

Mostly, I wanted to go find the six-year guys. I'd been with the Giants for six years and so had a lot of them. Simms was off with the press and would be for a long time. So I went looking for Burt and Byron Hunt and Harry and George and Lawrence Taylor.

When I finally found Lawrence, we just embraced, and then he looked at me and said, "It was worth it, Bill, you know? Damn, it was *all* worth it."

I found Byron Hunt. It had looked like he was going to be a full-out star when he came out of SMU, and he'd always been a damn good player for me and a team man and he could fill in all over the place. But he hadn't been a star. I liked him a lot.

Byron Hunt smiled and said, "You know, coach, I don't remember one bad day here. We ever lose any games in the past? 'Cuz I just forgot all those days."

Euphoria.

After a while, I made my way back to the place where the coaches dressed. Mickey Corcoran was there, of course. Mickey is always there. Mickey's just been there for me about thirty years.

Mickey said, "This one going home from here should be a little more pleasant than that one from Chicago last year, don't you think?"

I shook Mickey's hand.

"Thanks for everything, Mick," I said.

There was no rush to go anyplace now. Why do you want to leave the place in your career—hell, your *life*—where you've always wanted to be? Nobody wanted to let go of the day. The coaches showered and changed clothes. Nobody wanted to leave. We figured it could be as long as ninety minutes to the bus.

We just sat there and shot the bull about Super Bowl XXI.

It was a little more enjoyable than all those five-thirty staff meetings back at Giants Stadium in the middle of September.

It was probably one of the most enjoyable hours I've ever spent in my life.

Mickey kept talking about Simms. He said, "This is the biggest game of his life, and he just *showed up*, you know? You don't *ever* have to worry about that guy competing ever again."

A guy I know from the Raiders poked his head into the room and I asked him if Al had come to the game and he said, no, Al watched the game back at his hotel. And I wished Al could have been there in person, to see us do it. To see us join the club that not everybody gets to join.

Finally it was time to get on the bus. I took one more walk on the field. I'd probably be in the Rose Bowl again someday, for one reason or another. But then, maybe not. It was mostly empty now, like it had been when I'd shown up twelve hours earlier. There were just a lot of television crews and television lights sprinkled here and there around the end zones. Some Giants fans were still lingering up in the stands, wanting to hold onto the day like we did, and when we came out, they cheered.

I looked at those tight corners in the end zone.

They hadn't turned out to be much of a problem at all.

Neither had the sun.

The bus took us back to the hotel we'd spent the week in, a place called the Westin South Coast Plaza in Costa Mesa. It was about an hour ride. I sat in front, and watched this one chunk of California get eaten up by the bus, and spent most of the hour thinking back about all the roads that had brought me to Pasadena.

Because there had been a lot of them.

There was a party at the hotel. They had a big ballroom for Giants fans, old Giants players. A lot of my college teammates where there, friends I hadn't seen in quite a few years who came to the game. And it was a very emotional time. I mentioned earlier that Charlie Conerly seemed more affected by the victory than anyone. There were tears in his eyes when he congratulated me.

All these years, since the last championship, Giant quarterbacks who *didn't* win had had Conerly's name on their backs like a monkey.

Because he *had* won.

But the first thing Charlie said to me was, "I'm so

happy for Simms. Hell, I'm so happy for all of you."

It was as if the past and present had all crowded into this one big room.

Finally with the New York Giants, the past and present were getting along just fine.

I finally found my wife and my daughters and they were all just ecstatic. Wild, really, just *wild*. My youngest, Jill, had spent a little part of the day with actor Tom Cruise (another Jersey guy, another Giants fan). She'd also had her picture taken with Cruise.

I couldn't tell whether Jill Parcells was happier about meeting the guy from *Top Gun* or us getting to be top guns, as a matter of fact.

I finally got to bed at one o'clock in the morning, after a few beers. I knew I had to get up very early for one last Super Bowl press conference, which I did. And that afternoon we went to the airport for the flight back to Jersey. The Pro Bowl guys were going on to Hawaii, but the rest of us were going home.

The flight home was another party.

On the side of the plane, they'd painted "Super Bowl XXI Champion New York Giants!" It looked pretty good, I must admit. There were actually two planes going back, one for the families, the other for the coaches and the players and the administration and the staff. And on our plane the stewardesses were dressed up in Giants uniforms.

When we flew over Denver, our pilot got on the p.a. system and said, "If you look out the windows to your left, down below you will see the City of Denver, home of the Super Bowl XXI *RUNNER-UPS,* the Denver Broncos. Remember them?" The pilot's name is Augie Stascio, and he's from the Bronx, and he's a Giants fan, and he's become a good friend.

He got a big cheer with that stuff about the Broncos.

It was the middle of the night by the time we got back to Newark. Even when we've gotten back late in the past, we've had to get into some kind of traffic pattern. Not this time. Straight in.

Augie said, "This is the best treatment we've ever gotten in New York."

I said, "Why not, you know, Aug?"

The DC-10 was merely carrying the champions of the world.

You bet. Champions of the whole damn world.

23

Gatorade Man

Go ask the historians to find out when it was that Harry Carson first gave me one of those Gatorade showers. I honestly don't even remember.

But I guess those showers turned out to be symbolic, and told a lot more about me and the Giants than I ever could have told.

The showers showed I was one of them. They weren't planned or contrived or stagy; mostly they were just fun, and I went along with it. And I went along with it because I'm one of them.

I'm the guy in charge. I say yes and no, and when somebody has to get cut, I have to do it. When a player has to be confronted about drugs, I'm the guy who does the confronting. When the Giants went 3-12-1, I was the guy who nearly got fired.

But I am a Giant. We are in it together. The hardest thing for any coach or manager is to walk the line between being a boss, and also being someone the players know is their last line of defense. You are not born knowing how to do this. Some coaches don't care to do it. Some want to be disciplinarians all the way. They don't want to get out of the tower. God bless 'em. Good for them. If it works, go for it. I'm just not made that way. I like football players too much. I know you can't imagine seeing Papa Bear Halas underneath a wave of Gatorade, or Coach Lombardi, or Tom Landry. It wouldn't be them.

But it works for me. If it didn't, I would have stopped it after Shower No. 1. I would have pulled Harry Carson aside afterward and said, "Hey, cut the crap," or something poetic like that. I didn't. For me to stop it would have been phony. It would have been as phony as me stopping the joking with the guys in the offensive line, or getting on McConkey's case about being such a ham, or hanging around the weight room.

The reason I was so miserable in Colorado that year is because I was cut off from the world that defined who I am, really. I coach. I work in football. I like the hours. I like the people. Do I make a lot of money at it? You bet. More than I ever thought anyone would ever make in sports when I was starting out. And I'm talking about athletes. If somebody had told me at Hastings that any coach would make what I do now, I would have laughed. People love to speculate about what I was making from the Giants before the Super Bowl, and what I might make from here on out.

Well, go back to my answer to the people who wanted to know where Lawrence went to rehab.

None of your goddam business.

Let's just say that I'm able to support myself better than a backup shortstop in baseball, and less than one of those Michael Jordans in the NBA.

The Parcells are doing all right. All right?

But I did it for less—remember the $3000 contract at Hastings?—when I was a rookie, and I would do it for less now. What the hell is the point of doing this for a living if you don't like football players, and practice, and the locker room, and that feeling on Sunday morning, the one about "Are we gonna do it today"?

But I'll tell you this: The showers don't work for everybody. Over the winter, I saw some basketball coaches get nailed with Gatorade or ice or whatever, and it just didn't work.

Harry probably should have copyrighted the whole damn idea.

I've said that my father used to talk about all the guys he saw leave New York via Madison Avenue. I don't plan to leave coaching via Madison Avenue.

I don't do many endorsements or commercials, mainly because the money being offered doesn't make up for the time it takes away from me coaching my team. A lot of coaches like to do a lot of commercials. Not me. I think of time lost and say, "Nope."

I could do the commercials.

The money is out there. If I bit on everything that has been offered to me lately, I could make an extra $300,000 in 1987.

Not worth it.

You've got to get my attention with some large dough if you're going to get me away from Giants Stadium. And even if you get me away from Giants Stadium, you better guarantee that you need the minimum amount of time possible. If it's a television commercial, or a radio commercial, and you've got a couple of days in mind, forget it. Get me in, get me out, pay me and send me on my way.

I'm a pretty good salesman, as I've said. But I'm no dazzling personality. I don't think you'll see me mentioned as a replacement for David Letterman when he finally hangs it up.

I endorse the car I drive (now that's the sort of deal I like). I did a small sweater deal last season. I might do some business this season for a sporting goods outfit. I don't think you'll see my mug advertising a hell of a lot more.

I'd rather sit in my office with my remote control switcher and my cassette machine and try to spot something with the Redskins I never spotted before. Then I'd rather get up, make myself some bad coffee, go downstairs, see which of my players are hanging around the weight room—see if I can goose Benson or somebody like that.

Let's face it: I'd rather get doused by the Gatorade than bust my ass selling it.

O ne reason I didn't go commercial crazy, and endorsement crazy, after the Super Bowl is that I needed as much time as possible to get ready for the draft.

In the past, I had plenty of draft time. January was a fairly empty month, coaching wise, once we got bounced from the playoffs.

We didn't get bounced this time. This past January went all the way to the 25th of the month and that appointment with the Denver Broncos in the Rose Bowl.

We were going to pick last in the first round, and that's a challenge, but I hadn't gone to any of the all-Star games, I hadn't seen any of the players with my own eyes. Once I started concentrating on the draft after all the Super Bowl hullabaloo settled down, I felt like the whole world was a month or two ahead of me.

The draft is my responsibility. Mine and my scouts. Once one season ends, the assistant coaches are already getting ready for the next. They grade every possible aspect of the season that just ended, then they start looking at film of our opponents. I'm in touch with all that, wandering in and out of their offices.

But I'm thinking draft.

It's part beauty pageant and part crazy game show, the NFL draft. You evaluate the players, you bring some of them to your own stadium and work them out, you look at what they did in college, you look at their games, you talk to them.

If I'm serious about a kid, I want to talk to him. I want to get him in my office and look him in the eye and fire some questions at him and see how he responds. Sometimes after one of these meetings, I'll like a kid more than I did when I saw him on film.

Sometimes I'll make up my mind on the spot that I don't want him even trying out for my team.

I'm a people guy, you know that by now. I want to

know more than how much he can bench press and what his time is in the forty, and all that other crap. Numbers are important. But heart is as important to me. If heart isn't important, then there is no place for the Phil Mc-Conkeys in our game. I'm not saying that McConkey doesn't have talent, because he does, a load of talent, and all that toughness, and that spit-in-your-eye attitude of his.

But heart got him a Super Bowl ring. There are a hell of a lot of more talented people than McConkey who never got a ring.

I want to know about attitude and intelligence, and the ability to take it. I want to see how a kid reacts when he knows he's not going to step right in and be the star he was in college. Because very, very few of them step right in. I don't like to throw rookies to the wolves. Lawrence got right in there and ate the wolves, but Lawrence was different. Even Carl Banks came along slowly.

So in February and March I'm looking at college games we've had sent to us. I'm reading scouting reports, I'm talking to the scouts, we're examining what we need and what we think we can get down there in the basement of the first round, we're trying to guess how the first round will go. Because you never know. You think you've got it figured, you figure that the Eagles *have* to go for this guy and the Cardinals just can't pass on that guy, and they do, of course. They take the guy you hoped was still going to be available.

The week before the NFL draft is nuts. Don't talk to me. My wife likes to get out of the house. She knows I'm not going to tell her who we're picking. The reporters know better than to even ask. And then draft day itself is even more nuts, as you watch the thing unfold and change your own list of possibles. Once a player's gone, he's gone, and you better be ready to step right up with an alternative, because the draft is the lifeblood of the NFL.

And considering where we were picking this year, I thought the Giants did all right. We got a terrific wide receiver from Michigan State named Mark Ingram in the first round, and a safety from Florida named Adrian White in the second, and they're both going to help us.

I think.

But you never know.

The week after the draft is for second-guessing yourself.

By the time the draft is over, you can feel yourself moving toward next season. The euphoria of the Super Bowl is gone, if you've won the Super Bowl. If you've fallen short of the Super Bowl, but you did some good things, you're done patting yourself on the back for the good things you've done.

The assistant coaches are already thinking about game plans and tendencies.

The head coach is thinking about free agents he might want to look at, or even sign.

The press is wondering if you can repeat, if you've won, or whether it's your time to win, if you've never won.

The players are down in the weight room or out doing their running in the offseason conditioning program.

And July, when training camp officially opens, is on everyone's mind.

It is a nice time, because anticipation is taking the place of memories, especially if you're the Super Bowl champs. It is a good feeling for me to know as I sit in my office that my guys are downstairs working already. None of them were surprised the first day I poked my head into the weight room and said, "Any guys in here that still want to win? Wait. Let me put it another way: Any guys in here who *remember* how to win?"

They knew they were in next season.

I went up to Benson and said, "You still doing what it takes to be a little better than that sonofabitch across the line from you?"

Benson didn't like that too much.

I liked that he didn't like it.

Some days, I went down and said, "God takes it away sometimes right after He gives it to you, you know that, don't you?"

Then I just walked out the door.

I heard Benson yell, "Well, he hasn't taken it *yet,* okay?"

The day we got the new schedule, I was right down there with it, only because here were the New York Giants' first five opponents for the 1987 season:

Chicago Bears. In Chicago. Monday Night Football.

Dallas Cowboys.

Miami Dolphins.

San Francisco Giants.

Washington Redskins.

I said, "I take this as a pretty good opportunity for

us to find out by October if we're any freaking good."
And I told them to show up at training camp with their
jocks on.

I want to find out if Harry will need as much Gatorade this season as he did last.

24

Aftershocks, and Other Things

They barely had time to clean out Giants Stadium after our victory celebration the Tuesday after the Super Bowl.

Then the stories started hitting the newspapers that the Atlanta Falcons wanted me to come run their entire football operation and be the coach and make about $800,000 a year for doing all that.

There are some times in your life that are a little busier than others.

Three years before, three years and a month to be exact, I had been worrying about keeping my job with the Giants. Now I was the coach of the Super Bowl champs and the hot boy of the moment.

Funny business, right?

Were the stories about the Falcons true? My agent (and friend) Robert Fraley was sure they were, even if the Falcons hadn't done any tampering (I still had two years to go on my Giants contract). This is high finance. There are a lot of big boys out there. There are ways to get the word out that are well within the rules and don't make NFL commissioner Pete Rozelle fall on you the way a building would.

I was in Indianapolis for the big scouting party of college players; it was taking place at the Hoosier Dome. I was aware that this big media storm was going on about me, but I managed to stay out of the line of fire. I scouted players all day long at the Hoosier Dome. Then at night, I'd go have dinner with Bob Knight at this little old Italian restaurant that was one of his favorites.

When I'd finally get back to my hotel room, there would be about forty-eight messages from the press trying to get a response from me about it.

And I felt bad the story got out the way it did, because I felt the Maras and even George Young deserved to enjoy the glow of the Super Bowl without getting caught up in a shitstorm that was in no way their doing.

Still: I have become aware over the years that nothing is forever in the business of coaching. When the staff gets fired at Wichita State and you're on the staff, you go too. Nobody asks if it's going to be tough on your family, anything like that. It's the same everywhere. Somebody can make a decision with your life. I'd found out with the Giants in 1983. I'd seen what had happened with Dan Henning and the Falcons.

I saw it with John Mackovic in Kansas City last season. Make the playoffs and get fired? What the hell was *that*?

So we heard this offer was out there.

Robert Fraley asked the Giants for permission to talk to the Falcons, nail down the stories. It is Robert Fraley's job to be loyal to me and my family and not any team. Again, he is friend and agent, and sounding board, and support system. It is all part of his job. He thought it was good business to see what was out there.

The Giants said no.

Fraley went to the NFL.

Rozelle said no.

That was that.

Oh, you want to know if I would have gone to the Falcons if the Falcons had really wanted me and the offer had been real, right?

So do I, as a matter of fact.

I've heard people say since, "Oh, Parcells would *never* leave the Giants."

Well, I've learned not to say never in this business. I've been too many places, seen too many things. Hell, it might have gone down to the wire with the Falcons, like that Jeff Rutledge sneak in the Super Bowl. I would have had to decide whether to duck my head and run with the ball, or punt it away at the last second.

It is a crazy life, but I'm as happy as I've ever been. My wife Judy has been a constant elegance in my life, going all the way back to Wichita State. She has made the moves without complaint, always given us a wonderful home no matter what financial hardships she was working under, and when the time came to put her foot down in Colorado, she was absolutely right. It was for the best.

For us, for the family, maybe even for my career. Who knows how things would have turned out if I hadn't taken that year off?

My wife shows how you can be a wife and mother and still be a strong and independent and creative woman. She's not a big football fan. I think that is good. We don't talk a lot about football when I'm home, as a result. It's almost a running joke in the Parcells house.

Judy will ask me who we're going to draft first and I'll say, "None of your business."

It's worked so far. When one of my friends in the game drops a hint that they're going to make a trade and then won't tell me, it will drive me crazy. I'll complain about it to Judy, and she'll smile one of those knowing wife smiles and say, "Serves you right."

In a generation when sometimes you get the idea that the youth of this country is going to hell in a hand-basket, I have been blessed with three wonderful daughters, smart and independent as their mother. Jill is the last to go off to college; she'll be at Gettysburg. Suzy, who's married now, went to Idaho State. And Dallas is at East Carolina. They have seen the world and are better for it, I hope.

Of course, they don't know as much about football as they think they know.

There was a big flap when I didn't show up at the White House when the Giants went as a team to meet President Reagan; everybody tried to read things into it because of the business with the Falcons, and all the newspaper theories that I was having trouble hammering out a new contract with the Giants. (By the time you read this I might have a big contract extension and I might not. I won't lose any sleep over it. I figure I'll always be able to find work somewhere. I can go back to The Country Club of Colorado, right?) I just preferred to watch Jill go play a high school basketball game. I don't get a lot of chances to do that.

Besides, I'm not a social person.

I stink at golf.

I'm getting to be a better trout fisherman. I go down to the Manasquan River in Jersey with my pal Timmy Burke in June. He's a fishing captain who also does security work for the Giants.

Timmy's a good friend. So is George Hagler, who owns one of those Jersey coffee shops I talked about; George's family has only owned the joint for sixty-eight years.

I've been friends with Danny Astrella since we were kids. He is more than a friend actually; he is an inspiration to me. He's the youngest of fourteen children, son of parents who couldn't speak English. Poor family. They slept three in a bed when Danny was growing up. He started driving a truck when he was nineteen. He went to school and learned a little more about the trucking business. Finally he started his own company. It is known as Raiders Express. It is now a successful independent carrier on the East Coast.

Knight will be my friend for life. So will Al. And Mickey.

My brother Don, who's just twenty months younger than me, also lives in Jersey, works for the Marine Midlands Bank in New York City. Don was a hell of a back for West Point before I went there to coach. One of the most famous Army-Navy games in history was a quarterback duel between Rollie Stichweh of Army and this fellow named Roger Staubach of Navy in 1963.

Navy won because Army ended up at the Navy two-yard line when time ran out.

My brother Doug, who played at Virginia, lives in Oradell, teaches at a school there, runs a lot of recreation programs for the town. He umpires, he refs, he can't get enough of sports. None of the Parcells brothers got cheated in the energy department. My sister Debbie works as a secretary over in Montvale, New Jersey.

Jersey family. Family ties, you know?

I've never really left, not in my mind. It is why the Super Bowl championship was such an acute thrill for me. It's why I'd like for my guys to do it again. You've heard that repeating a championship in sports is the hardest thing to *do* in sports? Well, it is. There are a lot of reasons, some big, some small: Complacency, injuries, your luck runs out, things like that.
sons, some big, some small: Complacency, injuries, your luck runs out, things like that.

But the biggest reason is that the rest of the NFL will turn into snipers this season, and they'll all be shooting for the Giants. It's my job to figure out a way to dodge the bullets. I've been at this business a while now. I've been to Wichita State and Hastings and back to Wichita State. Been to Army and Florida State and Vanderbilt and Texas Tech. I was head coach at Air Force. Then I was out. Then with the Patriots and finally the Giants.

I've learned some things.

You can't *ever* have enough Gatorade, of course.

And you can't ever think winning is final.

Bring on the season.

INDEX ●

A

Adams, George, 12, 196
Air Force Academy, 2, 31, 52, 59
  course loads at, 62–63
  resigning from, 67
Allegre, Raul, 197, 207, 214
Ameche, Alan, 22
Anderson, Ottis, 111, 223, 235
Ard, Billy, 188
  in offseason, 199
Arizona State, 34
Army
  See West Point
Astrella, Danny, 257
Atlanta Falcons, 55, 103, 111,
  121, 253

B

Baltimore Colts, 66, 109
  and Bill Belichick, 186
  in championships, 2, 22
Banks, Carl, 49, 54, 92, 95, 98,
  136, 184, 197, 248
Banks, Ernie, 218
Barnes, Ronnie, 4–5
Basketball, 27, 154, 163
  Indiana University, 23, 26, 44
  See also Knight
Battle, Bill, 52
Bavaro, Mark, 92, 133, 187, 197,
  205–207
Beathard, Bobby, 211
Bee, Clair, 47

on drilling, 53
Belichick, Bill, 104, 186–188, 204
Bench, Johnny, 48
Benson, Brad, 10, 188, 199, 250
Berry, Raymond, 22
Bias, Len, 156, 159
Boston College, 63
Brown, Jim, 9, 145
Brunner, Scott, 102, 113–116
Bryant, Bear, 64–65, 102
Burke, Timmy, 257
Burt, Jim, 54, 92–93, 133, 190,
  205, 237
  and Joe Montana, 224

C

Cahill, Tom, 41, 51, 61
Carmichael, Harold, 99
Carpenter, Rob, 99, 102–103,
  105, 140
Carson, Harry, 1, 3, 14, 16, 26,
  54, 90, 96, 135, 141, 156–157,
  191
  and Cowboys, 196
Carthon, Maurice, 183, 190
Chicago Bears, 1, 84, 140–142
  preseason game with, 188–189
  in Super Bowl XX, 139
College All-Stars, 123
Conditioning, 130–132, 165
Conerly, Charlie, 21, 239–240
Contemporary Services, 13
Corcoran, Mickey, 22–28, 30, 45,
  142–143, 161, 237–238